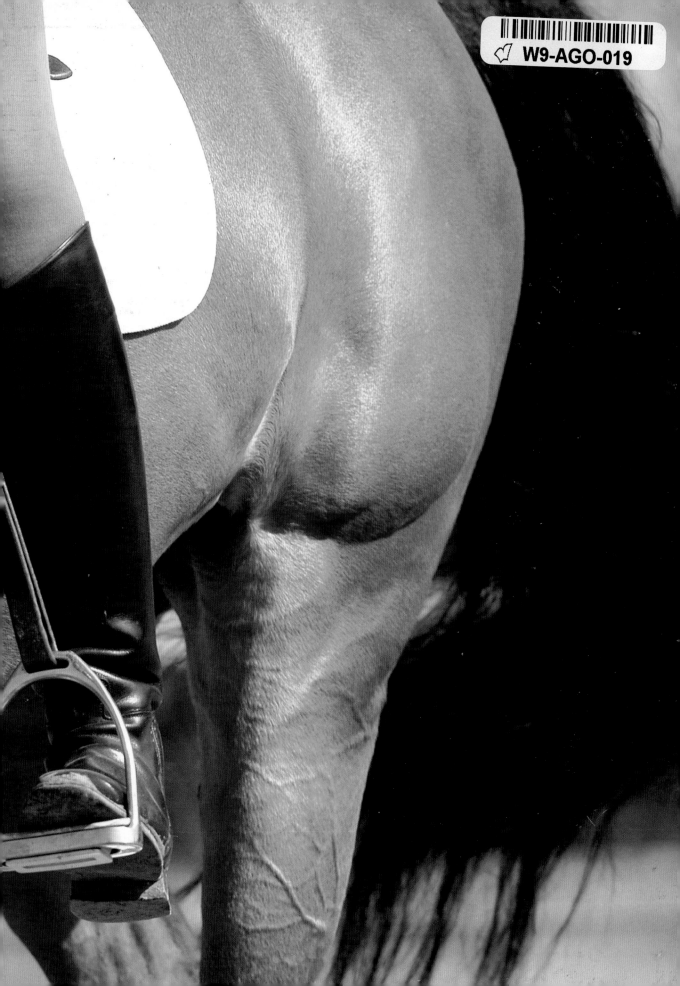

100 WAYS TO IMPROVE YOUR HORSE'S SCHOOLING

SUSAN McBANE

David and Charles

TO SUZIE, for being one of those dogs of
a lifetime, and JESS, her successor, who
is beating her own, very individual path
through life.

A DAVID & CHARLES BOOK
Copyright © David & Charles Limited 2006

David & Charles is an F+W Publications Inc. company
4700 East Galbraith Road
Cincinnati, OH 45236

First published in the UK in 2006

Text copyright © Susan McBane 2006

Susan McBane has asserted her right to be identified
as author of this work in accordance with the
Copyright, Designs and Patents Act, 1988.

A catalogue record for this book is available from the
British Library.

ISBN-13: 978-0-7153-2190-4
ISBN-10: 0-7153-2190-0

Horse care and riding are not without risk, and while
the author and publishers have made every attempt
to offer accurate and reliable information to the best
of their knowledge and belief, it is presented without
any guarantee. The author and publishers therefore
disclaim any liability incurred in connection with using
the information contained in this book.

Printed in Singapore by KHL Printing Co Pte Ltd
for David & Charles
Brunel House   Newton Abbot   Devon

Commissioning Editor: Jane Trollope
Art Editor: Sue Cleave
Desk Editor: Jessica Deacon
Project Editor: Anne Plume
Production Controller: Beverley Richardson

Visit our website at www.davidandcharles.co.uk

David & Charles books are available from all good
bookshops; alternatively you can contact our Orderline
on 0870 9908222 or write to us at FREEPOST EX2
110, D&C Direct, Newton Abbot, TQ12 4ZZ (no stamp
required UK only); US customers call 800-289-0963
and Canadian customers call 800-840-5220.

Contents

Roads to Rome

There are many different schooling systems. They may all work, but some work better than others, and with less stress on horse and trainer. To an extent, some methods/techniques may work better for some horses than others, given that all horses are different, but there are certain principles that are applicable to all, based on how horses think and learn and how their bodies work. Even abused horses can be largely 'brought round' if appropriate psychology and physical techniques are used.

Conversely, some systems appear to work superficially, but when they are really put to the test, it is found that the horse does not behave as required reliably. Some systems should also be rejected on the grounds of equine welfare; this might include those that

- frighten horses by using physical and psychological brutality and bullying;
- confuse them by, say, applying conflicting aids such as hands and legs simultaneously;

- make them feel insecure, as, for instance, in some elements of round pen work, or that force them into an 'overbent' posture of the head and neck which is physically uncomfortable and prevents them seeing clearly (because of the way their eyes work);
- force them to hold their bodies and move in any way that causes physical discomfort or pain and mental distress (including neglecting to develop the correct 'riding muscles').

You will find that some more complicated aspects of schooling theory and practice are missing from this book. This is because I feel there is a simpler way of obtaining a good result, and am writing this book for owners who are inexperienced in schooling and may have been having problems, or who don't know what to do next. A schooling/riding system must

- be based on how horses (not humans) think and learn, so as not to confuse the horse;

- have a logical progression of development – things to learn;
- be humane; and
- be uplifting for both onlookers and participants, human and equine.

Many people embrace, often either with relief or in desperation, any new or well promoted system simply because they do not have the knowledge, experience or the skill to rely on themselves. This is understandable, but it does not always solve their problems, because if you follow a system blindly you cannot accept, or even see, its shortcomings when you encounter difficulties.

The availability today of so many different methods of schooling, training, riding and groundwork is truly bewildering for most 'ordinary' horse owners, who may find it impossible to choose between them. For instance, there are several different 'natural horsemanship' systems training practitioners; there are individual trainers and clinicians of the same ilk; there are 'establishment' teaching organizations in different countries; discipline-specific methods such as in certain showing seats; and classical riding (which many claim to teach, but who in fact do not, in practice), and even different nuances of that. Furthermore, nowadays we also have increasingly the psychologically powerful scientific sector. The mushrooming of 'behavioural' therapists, trainers and theorists is, unfortunately, adding to the confusion, particularly as most non-scientifically trained or qualified horse owners and teachers are not familiar with correct scientific terminology and theory (and, most unfortunately, are often looked down upon, and even belittled, by those who are).

More seriously, some of the most highly qualified scientists disagree not only about practical techniques, but also about the very nature of how horses learn – and, of course, emphatically insist that they are right – and

scientists are supposed to be objective.

I have written this book to try to cut through all this confusion by presenting simple, logical techniques that I know work with a wide variety of horses and ponies, and that also comply with the four schooling/riding system requirements listed above. I hope and believe that it will solve a lot of your problems, that it will give you reliable information and help, and will also point you in supportive directions for progress (see also the Further Reading section at the end).

In the UK, it is becoming increasingly important for owners to be able to school their own horses, because good riding schools that provide a solid structure of training for riders and teachers, and often horses to sell, are becoming scarce. A knowledgeable and sympathetic teacher and/or trainer will always be invaluable, but the more effectively that you yourself can school your horse, the more independent, confident and fulfilled you will be.

Roads to Rome

Setting yourself up for success

There is no getting away from the fact that to be good at schooling horses you need to be a knowledgeable and competent handler and rider. For this reason this book is not aimed at novice riders, and it is assumed that you have, or are well on the way to acquiring, that basic essential, namely an independent, balanced seat, which means that you can stay on and in balance without gripping like a limpet (except in an emergency situation), and most certainly without hanging on to your horse's mouth (see Further Reading, for books to help improve your riding).

Being a trainer is an immense responsibility, and you really do need specific qualities, such as:

- respect for, and love of horses;
- self-control and discipline;
- the ability to concentrate wholly;
- detailed knowledge of how horses learn, of practical techniques and the ability to apply them correctly and consistently;
- commitment;
- sensitivity;
- kindness;
- the open-mindedness to continue lifelong learning.

It is said that the average mature horse has the mental capacity of a seven-year-old child. Maybe this is why the most successful schooling sessions are quite short – half an hour to 40 minutes should usually be enough. This is more beneficial and effective than longer, unproductive ones.

Remember that if your horse is uncomfortable he won't concentrate. His tack, his feet, his back, his mouth and the weather all affect him. I personally will not give lessons in bad weather: it puts off both horses and humans, and can give the horse unpleasant associations.

For yourself, keep fit, flexible and mentally relaxed. Do not train new exercises when you are tired, stressed or unwell. In fact, do not school at all – maybe go out for a gentle hack, if anything. Try to stay upbeat and positive –

then there's a good chance your horse will, too.

Although it can be very difficult when you keep your horse on a communal yard, do not let other people side-track or rush you. Some of the most confused horses I have been asked to teach are on these yards because their owners have not known who to believe and have therefore tried a bit of everything, to the detriment of their horse. Rely on a trusted teacher, and take your time.

General thoughts

Lifelong learning

We have already established that to be good at schooling you need to be a good rider. You cannot possibly hope to teach a horse *what you want him to know* without

- having a feel for what a horse is about to do, or at least being able to react appropriately, instantly;
- being confident;
- being able to apply accurate, effective techniques; and
- being able to apply them at the right time.

Cheer up! Even if you don't have all those qualities now, I hope you will have some, or all of them, by the time you've finished reading this book, because that is what it is for – to help you to improve your schooling, and so help you to develop these fundamental tenets of good riding. (See also Further Reading, p. 150.)

The reason I emphasized the words 'what you want him to know' above is because horses are learning all the time anyway: their evolution made them that way, and they learn just as quickly what you *don't* want them to do or know as what you do. Every little thing you do to a horse teaches him something, good or bad. If you poke your horse in the eye every time you put a headcollar on, or crush his gums and pinch his lips or tongue every time you bridle him, he will learn to become headshy.

Being prepared to embrace 'Lifelong Learning' wholeheartedly will vastly increase your confidence because you will know, and in time automatically apply, the most appropriate actions for given situations, and will learn not only how to deal with problems but also what to do next when schooling. Ride, read, listen and watch as much as you can, and this includes observing horses at liberty with each other.

Finding a skilled, empathetic trainer is a job in itself, but if you succeed, having such a trainer can be a godsend. Buy or borrow from friends or libraries as many books, videos, DVDs and CDs on riding, behaviour and schooling as you can, both old and new. So many true horsemen of yesteryear have left us their legacy of knowledge in their books. Consider any method which is not physically or mentally brutal. Be prepared to go to clinics, courses, lecture-demonstrations and lessons, and think through what you experience. (It is clear from the archaic attitudes of many very experienced horse people that their learning process has not progressed one iota since they first set eyes on a horse.)

You may think that all this will confuse you. However, if you are already a good rider (as we have mentioned), you should be able to identify the really good from the not-so-good, and use it accordingly. It is important to formulate your own philosophy eventually.

Remember, too, that the more techniques you have in your 'armoury' that are both effective and humane, the more horses you can deal with. If you want to become really good, don't just regard learning about horses as a hobby even if they aren't your living. Make it one of the most important things in your life.

1 Learn how horses learn

I have to start this very first topic with some bad news, which is that not all experts (scientists, academics or practical horsemen and women) agree on how horses learn. Some of the best qualified scientists, who are also equestrians, disagree and so do some of the most effective lay (non-scientific) horse people. They do all get results, but presumably in different ways.

So how do horses learn?

I promised that this book would be simple, and based on actual techniques (that would be explained) that I know work, and I will keep to this. Those who seek more detailed information about the various scientific angles of learning theory, terminology and so on, can read about them in other books (*see* Further Reading on page 150).

The thing about theories is that, proven or otherwise, they can have a 'that's the way it is' status one year, and be discredited the next. The behavioural sciences encompassing the questions of how horses learn continue to evolve slowly, and this includes the presentation of opposing opinions, often very firmly held. A contributor to *Equine Behaviour*, the journal of The Equine Behaviour Forum (p. 150), wrote that if highly qualified scientists cannot agree, where does that leave the rest of us, and does anybody really know? Personally, I don't think they do! The fact that horses can and *do* learn can probably best be explained in the following way: that there are

certain basics which apply to most of them, and that individual – perhaps genetically inherited? – propensities and also experiences colour their responses to learning situations.

It has long been a common tenet that horses can only learn by constant repetition. Certainly repetition does work, but we must all know of instances when a horse has learnt a lesson from only one association with, or experience of, something – such as a gate banging shut on him, or a rider beating him up in front of a fence or in a manège.

On a better note, horses often learn things for themselves if they are allowed the time to work things out independently. I was once watching an international four-in-hand team training at home, and they managed to get a back wheel of their carriage caught behind a tree they were going round in a fairly close-growing wood. The driver sat there silently and gave the horses their heads. After a moment, the wheeler nearest the tree indicated that he wanted to go backwards, then he and the other three horses reversed the carriage together, pulled further out round the tree, and carried on forwards, to profuse vocal praise from the driver.

Horses can clearly learn things both to their own advantage, and to ours. For instance, my friend's pony was persuaded to learn to stand still for, and after, mounting by being given a mint from the saddle once her rider was settled and ready for the off. Purists won't like this method but it is harmless and it certainly works. It may

not be 'discipline' but it is still 'training' of a sort.

So then, horses can, it seems clear to me, learn by repetition, by association, sometimes by imitation (but not 'stable vices'), by working some things out, by being shown things, by correction and by reward. As regards the latter two aspects of learning, there is considerable disagreement – of course! And it gets worse, in that some highly qualified, respected and experienced people cannot even agree on what constitutes reward.

So where does that leave us?

Let's keep things simple and logical. My own viewpoint puts me firmly in the camp of schooling horses basically along the lines of how they behave and learn in a herd, because this is how nature evolved their minds to cope – and it works.

If a horse does something

unpleasant to another of similar or superior rank (yes, I know some people believe that there is a hierarchy, and some don't) which the second horse does not like, the first is told about it *clearly and instantly*. If he is reasonably intelligent, he won't do it again – well, maybe only once. Conversely, if he gives pleasure to another horse by, say, mutual grooming, tail-flicking (fly-removal services) or supportive companionship, the other accepts and usually returns it, even if the second horse is very superior, as may often be the case. (As in humans, where friendship or love is concerned there's no accounting for taste!)

This translates as meaning that horses need boundaries, to know what is acceptable/wanted and what is not acceptable/not wanted. Keeping to this clear, fundamental 'school (or schooling) rule' makes learning and life with humans easier for horses to understand. You don't have to get complicated about things in order to be successful.

2 Understand how a riding horse should go

We all know that it is not natural for a horse to carry weight on his back. In practice, horses adapt well to it mentally if it is introduced humanely and gradually. Physically, it can be a different matter if trainers do not understand basically how the skeleton and muscles function, and do not teach the horse to develop the correct posture and muscles for carrying weight safely.

attached by tendon tissue to its bones. Put simply, imagine two bones with a joint between them. A muscle will be attached to one bone at one end, and to the other at its other end. When a nerve message tells the muscle to shorten (contract), this causes a pull on the second bone, moving it from the joint between them.

The importance of the vertebral bow

Looking at a horse's skeleton from the side, you will notice that the backbone has a very slight upward bow or arch

The horse's physical structure

The horse's body is founded on his skeleton of living, hard but non-rigid bone, plus gristly cartilage with more 'give' in it for cushioning between joints. The bones are held together and supported by tough, fibrous bands, sheets or cords of fibrous tissue called ligament. It is strong and sensitive but only very slightly elastic: when injured by being over-stressed, it takes months to heal.

The backbone is made up of a line of complex-shaped bones called vertebrae. Each is hollow through the middle and, with the bones lying end to end as they do, this forms a tunnel down which the soft spinal cord (nerve tissue) runs from the brain to part-way down the tail. Nerves branch off from it between the many vertebrae.

The skeleton also has many muscles

shape; this is a stronger structure for carrying weight than a straight or downward shape. The horse's heavy abdominal contents are slung partly from the underside of the spine by membranes, but when carrying a rider, weight is also borne from on top, which flattens the spine somewhat, stretches the ligaments beneath it, and weakens the structure.

You also see that the horse's neck vertebrae form a shallow letter S tipping towards the horse's head, its lowest curve passing down between the shoulder blades. The S is the right way round seen from the right, the wrong way from the left.

Further back in the hindquarters, there are five vertebrae fused together to form a bone called the sacrum. The joint between the front of the sacrum and the lumbar vertebra in front of it is the lumbosacral joint and is at the point of the croup. Flexing this joint enables the horse to reach further forwards with his hind legs and engage his hindquarters (see below, left).

How it works

This engagement is brought about by the contraction/shortening of various muscles attached around the skeleton, but particularly to the undersides of the loin and hindquarter part of the vertebral column, to the pelvis and thigh bones, and to the back of the breastbone at one end and the pelvis at the other (the abdominal muscles). This collective action raises the spine and tilts the bottom of the pelvis forwards (the horse lifts his back and tucks his bottom under). Furthermore, muscles under the lower neck vertebrae also shorten,

raising the bottom of the neck, which pushes the neck and head forwards.

Put very briefly, the horse is then going with 'both ends down and the middle up', enhancing the vital vertebral bow so that the body becomes, with continued muscle use, better able to carry your weight, and so to work with less likelihood of injury caused by weight-bearing (see above).

You will find out how to achieve all this later in this book (*see* pages 62 and 63).

3 Use your voice correctly

Horses are not very vocal creatures. They communicate mostly by body postures and actions, and also, I am sure, by mental imaging. They use their voices sometimes, of course, in screams (mainly stallions), roars for want of a better word, neighs, whinnies, squeals and whickers. One thing is certain, they are extremely responsive to the human voice.

A lost opportunity?

It seems that not permitting the use of the voice in dressage competitions stems from the days when horses were used in warfare, when often horse and rider had to move across country as silently as possible. Then it was essential for the horse to obey aids by feel, not sound, as the sound of the human voice would have alerted the enemy.

It is unfortunate that this practice has persisted in dressage – though it hasn't anywhere else, including in the tests of the Classical Riding Club (p. 150) – particularly as it has a disadvantageous knock-on effect in that many people, I find, do not even use the voice when they school, partly because they feel that the horse must get used to working without it, and

partly because they feel that it is wrong or cheating!

Well, I could not disagree more. Circus and driving horses all rely greatly on the voice, and it is a very real help in schooling and in generally communicating the mood of a situation to a horse. It is most important to learn to use your voice effectively in all situations. There is nothing at all wrong, of course, in quietly chatting away to your horse in a friendly way. Even then, you'll notice that he is listening out for specific words which he connects with particular things, such as movements or events in the day – words like 'over' or 'carrots'.

The effects of sound

First, remember that as far as your horse is concerned, whatever you say

is just a sound. Imported horses soon learn English commands, often within days or a very few weeks. The lilt of a particular accent can take a horse back to good or bad times with consequent changed behaviour. And music has the same effect: a circus horse only has to hear familiar music to perform his act to it unbidden by his trainer. Dressage horses nearly always remember their 'to music' tests, and parade and display horses often become animated when they hear music through loudspeakers.

What can I do?

Always be sure to use the same command for a particular thing. If you want your horse to walk, say 'walk on' (therefore if he's trotting and you want him to walk, don't say 'whoa', say 'walk on'). If you want him to trot, for example on the lunge, say either 'terr-ot' *or* 'trot on' – but do not then keep saying 'trot on' when he already is, because to him this is another command, and he could become unsure what to do. Basically, don't keep giving a command when the horse is already complying, because if he's already doing it, he could become confused.

The tone of your voice is also important. I am a firm believer in teaching horses that 'no', spoken more or less sternly depending on the 'misdemeanour', means a correction, and 'good boy' or 'good girl' spoken with a pleased, inflected tone of voice means praise.

4 Don't worry about time off

It is said that herbivores (not just elephants) have infallible and lifelong memories – in other words, they never forget *anything*. This may be because their lives can depend on remembering good or bad situations and places. Compared with humans, horses' memories are phenomenal. This can be a good or bad thing; this section is about a good one.

to develop. This frequently results in horses performing that particular task much better than when they were first taught it and asked for it. This is probably why some trainers say that two schooling sessions a week learning new work are enough, although others prefer very short daily sessions (ten or twenty minutes). I prefer the former.

What about losing fitness?

It takes about three weeks of not working for an athletically fit horse to noticeably start losing physical fitness, so again, breaks of a couple of weeks or so are not a drawback. On the contrary, I feel that many competitive riders do not rest their horses enough. After hard, strenuous work such as racing or a high-level endurance competition or three-day event, it takes at least three weeks for a horse to recover properly, and that is if he were only reasonably tired, as opposed to exhausted.

I think not enough attention is paid to mental exhaustion as well as the physical sort: the psychological recovery from hard work takes time, as does the physical recovery of the brain and the stress placed upon the nervous system, not just the muscles and the rest of the body.

From both a schooling and fitness viewpoint, horses are more likely to benefit from fairly short breaks than to be disadvantaged by them.

Will my horse forget his lessons if he has time off?

A horse will never forget any of his schooling for as long as he lives. There may come a time when, due to age, injury, or lack of fitness after a long lay-off, he cannot actually do what you are asking, but he will certainly remember what you want and how to do it, even if he can't oblige – and if he can, he will. I once saw a circus horse perform without hesitation a trick he had not been asked to do

for five years. And I knew an old Thoroughbred ex-racehorse who had been lunged in a very specific way by a particular trainer when very young, and who was returned to her in retirement. Before an audience of about 50 members of the Equine Behaviour Forum, she lunged him her way as a demonstration of behaviour and memory, and he remembered everything perfectly.

Very often, a short break (a few days) gives a horse time to assimilate lessons, and allows certain structures in the brain relating to understanding

5 Do not force results with tack or training aids

There are so many competitions to go to these days. Some disciplines that once had seasons can now carry on all year round, and there are points to be gained, trophies to be won and rosettes to collect continuously. It is very tempting to take short cuts in training by using gadgets or training aids, indeed it is the norm in many professional competition yards.

What's wrong with training aids?

It does depend on the item concerned, but many give a false feel to the trainer because the horse is not responding normally, but going in an artificial way induced by the equipment.

There are three items I have used very occasionally when faced with really resistant horses, and these are the Chambon for groundwork, and the de Gogue or the Market Harborough for ridden work. All these remind the horse to lower his head if he raises it too much, but when he carries it correctly they have no effect *provided* they are correctly adjusted.

I do not feel the need for more coercive items such as running reins, draw reins or 'whole-horse' devices, and am horrified by people who adjust and use them harshly to force the horse into an often incorrect 'outline' or 'frame' (see posed photo, right). Not only is this treatment cruel, in my view, because it is distressing and probably painful, but it is also counterproductive because it does not result in correctly developed musculature, nor does it teach the horse to go with a self-maintained, correct posture. Furthermore, I so often hear that when you remove the training aid the horse goes just as 'badly' as he did before, or even worse.

I have also had experience of horses who subsequently developed behavioural problems once they felt free to go more naturally, and that the rider or handler was not in control. This is a human problem, not an equine one. The trainer needs to develop their assertive attitude, and their knowledge of humane, effective techniques.

What should I do?

- Teaching your horse to lower his head on verbal command is the best start (see p. 36). A voluntarily low head means a mentally and physically relaxed horse. In early schooling from ground or saddle, a horse should work with his poll about level with his withers – and always with his nose in front of the vertical.

- Always use the simplest, and the least gear with which you can obtain a result.

- Allow the horse time to mentally absorb his lessons and physically develop into his work, then you will have long-lasting, correct results and a contented, co-operative horse – most of the time!

6 Be prepared to reassess if you meet a problem

Horses and humans are flesh and blood, and we are all different; we are essentially individual and unique creatures. A major problem is that horses cannot tell us in our language when they are having difficulties, or when a particular request or job is incomprehensible to them, too hard or beyond their capabilities, or if they feel unwell. As always, the onus is on us to stop and think.

How can I tell if my horse is just being stubborn?

There is no doubt that, despite what some behavioural therapists and practitioners say, some horses blatantly take advantage of certain people. If he is your horse and he is playing you up, you need to be really firm and not stand for any nonsense, before he starts creating all sorts of other 'no-go' areas and you end up being completely dominated by him.

A natural horseman friend of mine (not the modern genre of 'horse whisperer' or natural horsemanship enthusiast, but a born, real horseman) told me many years ago to feel the neck of a horse who was giving me a hard time. He maintained that if, when he was misbehaving, his neck was hard and tight and especially if he was trembling, he was frightened; but if his neck was loose, soft and

relaxed he was having me on. I have used this test many times since to good effect, and am happy to pass it on to you. Another sign of your horse checking you out is if he starts playing up at some simple task he has accomplished without fuss several times previously.

If the task is new and the horse genuinely seems unable to grasp or perform it, always be prepared to return to the previous stage and confirm that it is properly established. Be ruthlessly honest with yourself, and be sure that the horse is developed and fit enough for the job, that the way you are asking him is absolutely correct, and that there are no worrying or exciting external circumstances that could be distracting him.

It is also most useful to have knowledgeable friends, contacts and a teacher to ask for ideas. You don't have to follow them, but an outside view can often be helpful. Also consider the next topic.

17

7 Make sure your horse is free of pain

It seems that horses generally have a low pain threshold. Maybe this has to do with their being prey animals, but pain and discomfort distract and affect a horse extremely quickly. Some bear pain stoically but become withdrawn and depressed, whilst others start apparently being difficult at the smallest irritation, which, unlike us, they are often powerless to get rid of.

How does a horse show that he is in pain?

Certain physical changes, and changes in behaviour or personality, will indicate that a horse is in some degree of pain; any of the following signs might indicate that something is distressing or hurting him:

- A change in demeanour: he becomes dull and/or distracted, or he may start performing some stereotyped behaviour or 'stable vice' such as weaving, rocking, head-tossing or standing awkwardly, trying to relieve the painful part (this is not necessarily a leg).
- Patchy sweating.
- The skin of the face is drawn tight, and the nostrils are wrinkled up and back, often with a 'sucked in' appearance immediately above them.
- Dull, sunken eyes.
- He looks tucked up in the belly and loin area.
- He stands with his head down, away from other horses, looking withdrawn and uninterested.
- A horse in severe pain will often groan and/or thrash about.
- Under saddle, he is unwilling to work, performance is poor, he is lacking in energy.
- Increased heart/pulse rate at rest.

What can I do?

The person you should first turn to for help is your vet. In the UK, a vet is the

only person legally allowed to diagnose injuries and illnesses in animals, although he or she may well refer your horse to another type of specialist, if appropriate, such as a physiotherapist or specialist farrier.

It is most important that anyone responsible for a horse (their own or someone else's) becomes really 'tuned in' to the horse's feelings as evidenced by his demeanour and behaviour; if they are concerned that the horse 'doesn't look right' they should never just pass it off as him just having an 'off' day. Spotting trouble very early on, before you are even sure, is the very best way to safeguard his health and well-being.

It is also important that you are confident about your horse's normal vital signs, including temperature,

pulse and respiration rates, and are competent to check them. Any good equine first aid book or general veterinary book should set out this information.

The areas to check first are the fit and adjustment of the horse's tack (pp. 28–9), the teeth and mouth, the back, limbs and feet.

Teeth and mouth: A vet or equine dental technician will be able to sort out any teeth or mouth problems. Teeth can make a tremendous difference to a horse's comfort, health and attitude. Sharp edges on the inside and outside of, respectively, the horse's lower and upper cheek (back) teeth, also hooks on the lower, very back teeth and the upper, front cheek teeth, can cause considerable injury

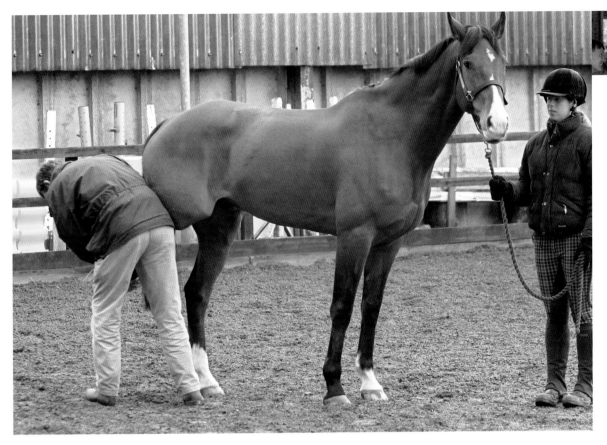

and pain when he is eating or working under saddle. Wolf teeth (small front cheek teeth) can cause pain or irritation, and youngsters often have very sore mouths when teething. In addition, growths can occur in the mouth, and teeth can be misshapen, broken or missing, or a milk tooth may be jammed on top of the permanent tooth.

Back problems: Pain and discomfort in the back is very often caused by a badly fitting saddle. If it is too tight it will pinch and restrict the circulation, resulting in muscle atrophy or 'shrinkage', usually below or behind the withers. If it is too wide it will shift about and cause pressure or friction injuries. Uneven or lumpy stuffing is an often overlooked problem, causing bruising and uneven pressure. A numnah under a saddle that is already too tight will only make the situation worse; however, it may offer a temporary solution with an over-wide one. An ill-fitting girth – for example, one that digs into the horse's flesh

behind the elbow, as above (which the rider cannot actually see from the saddle) – is a frequent cause of a horse not going freely, if not of girth

galls. A qualified saddle fitter should be consulted as soon as possible.

An ill-fitting rug can also cause bruising, usually of the withers and shoulders; also the chest.

The limbs and feet: Any problem in this area is the province of the vet and/or farrier. Expressions describing a horse as being 'unlevel', 'pottery', 'going feeling', 'not quite right' and so on, are all horse-world euphemisms for *lame*, the horse owner and rider's nightmare! Nevertheless, a horse is either sound or he is lame, although there are, of course, degrees of lameness.

To sum up

If a horse is in discomfort or pain there is no point in schooling. It is inhumane to use him and, in any case, he will not concentrate sufficiently on his work and could develop bad associations with it. The only solution is to try and identify the problem, and find a cure.

8 Vary the work routine

It is very sad to see that horses nowadays lead much more restricted lives than was the case years ago. Many horses and ponies seem to spend most of their working life in a manège or competing, often with little or no turnout time. This is an awful life-style for horses, who have a much more amenable temperament when they have a more varied, natural life-style. Let's look at some options.

Hacking

Horses nowadays often do not hack out, and this is a great pity because hacking can be really enjoyable, even if you have to box to another area to do it. The almost universal reason is that the roads (well, the road-users) are not safe; though having said that, there are many horses and ponies who *do* hack out sensibly and safely – and if police horses can be taught to be safe in all circumstances, so can others. In the UK, the British Horse Society runs riding and road safety courses and tests to help. Also, if you can persuade your nearest mounted police branch (or one of their retired personel) to run short courses in training and safety procedures, this would be an excellent schooling topic.

A change is as good as a rest

Make your horse or pony into a multi-disciplinary mount. Most horses enjoy a change, and it also has a great settling effect on a horse's mind to get to grips with different jobs. I believe that all dressage horses, for instance, should be able to at least pop over little cross-poles, and certainly they should be hacked out whenever possible. Hunting, of course, has always been regarded as a cure for stale and sour show and competition horses or racehorses; in the UK there is the new-format hunting, drag-hunting, or farm park rides. You don't have to jump if you really daren't – but how about a few lessons?

Groundwork

The type of groundwork that makes horses think is really good for them (this obviously excludes charging round and round on the lunge). I am a particular supporter of the Tellington Touch Equine Awareness Method (TTEAM), and often use aspects of it when teaching. Problem-solving and learning on the ground greatly help a horse's mental processes when he is under saddle.

In the manège

Vary your work, and don't always work on the same things. Also, don't always feel you have to teach your horse something new every time – but don't, either, repeat familiar work *ad nauseam*, as this is a sure way to sour and bore your horse. Probably the most boring thing you can do when schooling is to trot round and round the outside track achieving little or nothing.

9 Don't rush into new methods

I am all for learning as much as possible, but you have to be selective. Many years ago I had an instructor for a while who changed her methods every time she attended a course, lecture, or demonstration, or read a different book. Predictably, all her horses and riders ended up confused, puzzled, dissatisfied and even somewhat angry. This is not a good learning environment!

'There's nothing new under the sun'

This old saying has a lot of truth in it. As far as horses and ponies are concerned, they are basically the same now as when they were domesticated 6,000 years ago, and for a few million years before that. What has always worked will always work.

Probably the latest people to learn about horses are the native Americans who have had to do with them for only about four hundred years. The horses they captured were already trained, having come from the conquistadors and earliest settlers, but there was no one to teach the 'Indians' how to ride them, what aids to use, how to tend these new, strange animals to best effect, or how to teach the youngsters they bred to carry a rider or a pack, or pull a travois. Yet only two hundred years after their adoption of horsemanship, Custer described them as the finest light cavalry on earth.

How you can help yourself

Natural feel, common sense and a level of natural talent and intelligence can go a very long way. If you have a reasonable feel for horses and a good idea of what you and your horse need, you can teach yourself a lot by absorbing and assessing techniques and systems from books, videos and DVDs, and *selectively* trying them out after due consideration.

For those not quite so blessed, try to find a teacher and a system that really seem to help you and your horse, and give them a fair chance. Chopping and changing may be necessary in the early stages of your search, but this can be minimized by asking around for details of teachers in your area who sound likely to suit you. In this way, you are more likely to be able to be consistent in your ways with your horse. Don't hesitate to abandon what is clearly dubious or forceful: try new things that sound promising, but only keep them if they produce genuinely better results than those that you were using before.

Probably the two greatest qualities to cultivate are the ability to recognize when you are having a real problem that you cannot solve yourself, and that of being able to put yourself truly in your horse's position and see his life with *his* eyes, not your own human ones. Considering things in this way can be very revealing!

10 Keep warm in winter

Winter weather brings different conditions in different regions. Almost everywhere, though, it means colder weather – sometimes extremely cold. Working a horse in cold weather can bring its own special problems. There is good reason to believe that horses feel the cold less than humans, but they are certainly not immune to it.

How do cold temperatures affect a working horse?

Horses are mammals like us and feel and react to cold in just the same ways. When they are cold their coat hair stands up to increase the layer of warm, insulating air next to the skin. If this is not effective (such as when the hair is wet or the horse clipped), they shiver and the blood supply in the outer parts of their bodies diminishes as it is diverted to the body core, to maintain its temperature and the health of the vital organs.

This 'stiffens' up the muscles and other tissues, and without an ample blood supply they are in no state to perform demanding work, being likely to become more easily over-stressed, torn and injured. From the rider's point of view, if their own muscles are in a similar state they too are not working properly, which means that technique and riding skills suffer, and control and safety are compromised.

What can I do?

If you are going to work in weather that is wet as well as cold, particularly if your horse is clipped, consider using a waterproof exercise sheet on him to cover the back and hindquarters. If the weather is dry but cold, and maybe windy, use a warm exercise sheet (I still prefer wool), its weight depending on whether or not the horse is clipped over his back and the thickness of his natural coat (see right). If competing, remove it at the last possible minute.

For yourself, use warm gloves and socks under boots big enough to take the extra thickness so your feet are not squeezed and cold. Use rubber or synthetic stirrup treads which are warmer than metal. Wear a riding-style coat long enough to protect your thighs, particularly in wet weather.

Whether hacking or working in a manège, walk out for a good five minutes, then start slow jogging before progressing to trot, and warm up for at least ten minutes on a *loose* rein so that the muscles can stretch and the body can limber up. Introduce a gentle canter soon after this in order to get the horse warm.

11 Finish on a good note

Ideally, every schooling session would go beautifully, your horse would understand you perfectly, and you him. You would have no arguments or misunderstandings, and your planned work would be achieved with noticeable progress. Of course, it doesn't always go like that, but finishing with bad feeling on either side does not enhance your relationship.

Isn't it important that I always 'win', though?

No. Most horses are not confrontational by nature. Pain and discomfort apart, if horses do not do what their trainers ask (and this develops into an argument), it is usually because

- the trainer is not using a logical progression in schooling;
- earlier lessons leading up to the requested movement have not been properly taught, understood and absorbed until they become habits;
- the trainer is asking in a way which is not clear to the horse, or is actually preventing him from complying, such as by forcing an incorrect way of going.

Many of the problems I come across when teaching and schooling are caused by the horse's confusion and misunderstanding. This is often because their owners, past or present,

- have not instilled basic manners (safe behaviour);
- do not engender trust from the horse;
- expect horses to think like humans; and
- do not have the knowledge or skill to apply the aids correctly and clearly.

These factors can all lead to a rapid degeneration in temper-control, concentration, understanding and performance, and an increase in anger, desperation, mistrust and defensiveness. For the trainer to be 'determined to win' at any cost can be both dangerous and counter-productive.

What can I do?

Stop mentally, walk or lead the horse around on a long rein, and get things into perspective. Calm down, jolly him along (but don't praise him). Try again and reduce your request to start with. *Be delighted with even the tiniest bit of success, even a hint of movement in the right direction or in the right way.* Praise your horse instantly and finish. Next time you will almost certainly do better.

If you can't even manage this, go back to the previous stage in training, achieve a good result at something familiar, praise your horse warmly (not by thumping him but stroking and verbal praise) no matter what temperature your blood is – and stop.

Read up on what you are asking for, make absolutely certain, with an open mind, that you are doing things right, and for the long term, find a compatible trainer.

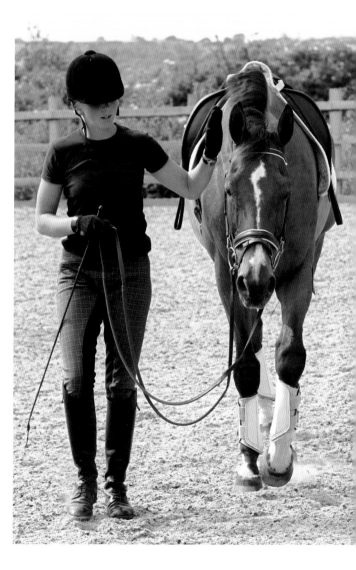

Be prepared

A helpful start

Many older readers (if there are any!) will remember when a prepared manège for riding was almost unheard of for 'ordinary' riders and horse owners. Even small riding schools didn't often have them (I started off in a sandy field and on Blackpool beach), and indoor schools were the preserve of formal academies and schools, the Services, and very wealthy private owners.

The point of this is to emphasize that a prepared manège or indoor school is not essential – but it really *can* be a help. A great deal of good work can be achieved out hacking, but a school with a good surface and, ideally, markers, makes life very much easier. Used to excess, though, it can sap the nerve of both horse and rider in that school work won't necessarily build confidence – to be a well rounded pair you need to get out and about and follow multi-disciplinary schooling or cross-training.

Horses' feet and legs evolved to operate on old grassland or turf – grass with a generous cushion of root mat beneath it. This provides just the right amount of cushioning to absorb the concussion caused by the horse's natural weight, and of springback after each step. The nearer you can get to turf the better, and it *is* possible to create an 'economy' manège (turfed or otherwise) without a membrane (see Further Reading p. 150, *The Horse Owner's Essential Survival Guide*).

Most manège surfaces nowadays, I find, are too deep: this may be seen as economical when putting down the surface (so you don't have to change it too soon), but it is difficult and discouraging for horses to work on, and can lame them through muscle strain and ligament and tendon damage. On the other hand, hard, thin surfaces cause concussion problems. The ideal is for the hoof to cut into the surface by about 1in (2.5cm). Drainage and harrowing are important, too, so that the surface is not inconsistent, with boggy and hard patches. Correct levels of sand and rubber seem to work well once well harrowed in and used, but sand alone (common because it is cheap) is not good: it has no spring in it at all, and if it is too deep, it is very heavy when damp or wet, and slides around when dry.

Ideally, you need the following for schooling your horse:

- a good surface;
- peace and quiet (no distractions);
- safe fencing in which you cannot catch your outside foot, and which will keep your horse in safely, should he get away;
- a reasonable space for your size and scope of horse: really an area of 40 x 20m is a minimum standard;
- safe equipment, such as jump stands and poles with no splintered wood, protruding bolts, screws and nails, no litter around or abandoned farm machinery;
- reasonable access to the manège, or a safe field or hacking route, even if it means travelling there.

12 Plan and prepare individual sessions

Being advised to plan your schooling session does not mean that you should be inflexible. Your horse is a living creature who may present you with unexpected problems that need addressing. Many people, though, do go into a manège with no real idea of what to do. The general plan suggested here will give you a guide to a session format to get you going correctly.

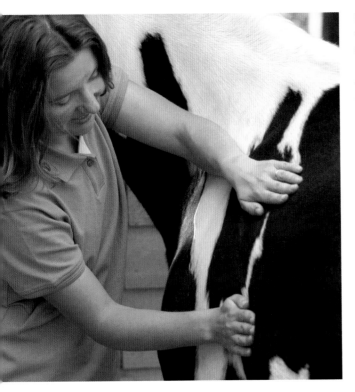

Pre-ride preparation

I believe in energy therapies and bodywork, and recommend that you stroke your horse fairly firmly all over, hand over hand, always with one hand on, to get the energy flowing and to stimulate his skin and muscles, as above. Then do some *gentle* stretches of the legs and neck to loosen them up. This would take ten minutes.

Schooling session format

1 Warm up: The idea of a warm-up is to get the blood flowing freely through the muscles. For this to happen, the muscles must be loose and unrestricted, so, on as loose a rein as you dare and ideally just holding the buckle, walk, then trot, and finally canter around the track and on large circles on both reins. This would take ten minutes.

2 Work in: This involves suppling and strengthening work, gradually bringing the horse into hand, getting him to accept the bit lightly in self-balance with his head and neck long, low and *in front of* the vertical, also raising his back and reaching forwards with his hind feet. Use all three gaits and some basic lateral movements, if the horse can do it, to open up the shoulder and hip joints and work the muscles on both the inside and outside of the legs. Rest your horse by walking or standing on a free rein, with the reins held at the buckle so that he can really stretch down and rest. This would take ten minutes.

3 Work Now comes the time for any current or new work which has not been mastered. This would take ten minutes.

4 Cool down Cool your horse down by walking on a free rein in small part-circles so that his outside foreleg crosses over his inside one, asking with your outside leg for some bend round your inside leg; this is achieved by using your seat, legs and eyes (see pp. 52–4). Do part-circles to left and right, weaving your way around the school to the gate. This gently stretches the muscles on both sides of the horse after work.

Post-ride care and checks

Hand-rub your horse to help dry him, if he is damp, then ideally give a full grooming (body brushing), and finally wisp him – an old practice akin to massage – or massage him to treat his muscles. Also, do some stretches (See the horse's health books, Further Reading p. 150.)

Is all that really necessary?

I certainly believe that the four stages of a schooling session *are* necessary, and that the pre- and post-ride parts are of great benefit. This will all show in a blooming, contented and correctly developed horse who will be a real credit to you.

13 Assess your horse accurately

It can be very tricky and difficult to assess your swan accurately, and to have to admit that he has at least *some* rather more goose-like qualities! Never mind: no horse is perfect. Understanding his faults and problems is the best basis for formulating a personalized schooling programme aimed at accentuating the positive and improving the negative.

Know what you're dealing with

It doesn't matter whether you are aiming at Olympic glory, winning at your local riding club or wanting to produce an amenable, manoeuvrable hack, you cannot school a horse beyond the very basics (which are not enough for safety and pleasure) unless you know his strengths and weaknesses. These can be physical and psychological.

Physically, first of all you need to assess your horse's conformation when he is standing still. Then assess how easily he copes with movements such as backing, turning, doing small circles, scratching his hip with his teeth or his ear with his hind foot, rolling, getting up and down and so on; and you should also consider his action, ridden and loose (see bottom right), and when jumping, to get a full picture.

Psychologically, you need to be sure you know his personality – for example, does he need you, or does he have a secure inner world of his own? Is he constantly screaming after his friends when separated? Does he show any stereotypies? Does he get on with other horses? Is he basically a leader or a follower? Is he interested in working, or is he a shirker? – that sort of thing.

What do I do then?

Once you have a clear assessment of these things, you can then work out a programme of physical and psychological/behavioural schooling to enhance his positive traits and improve his negative ones. Nothing will improve if you don't do this. Nothing you do will change your horse's inborn, inherited personality and temperament, but you can improve his behaviour by management and training, and build up his musculature to disguise conformational faults to some extent, and enable him to work well for you.

Try objectively to assess your horse yourself. Don't make excuses for him. See him as he is, and write everything down – and be absolutely truthful. You can compare notes with friends, but it is a great help to call in an empathetic, knowledgeable expert who will assess your horse physically and psychologically.

This can be done through watching the horse at liberty with others, during loose, in-hand or ridden work, and in the stable. An experienced person with a feel for horses will give you an opinion in an hour, probably less.

14 Adjust your tack logically and humanely

Be prepared

You may well be thinking: 'How boring! I know how to put tack on.' Of course, but do you just follow what everyone else does, or what someone has told you, or do you really think through the effect that your horse's tack has on his body and mind, his reaction to your aids, and his willingness and ability to move well and correctly? Distressed, uncomfortable horses do not learn well.

Think about how tack should fit

Precisely how tack should fit is covered in more detail in other horse books (*see* Further Reading p. 150). For now, I hope the following will prove helpful.

The bridle

The bridle's purpose is to hold the bit in place. Many bridles, nosebands and bits are fitted far too tightly today in the mistaken belief that this gives more control and 'makes' the horse go 'correctly'. In fact it has become such an all-pervading fashion that most people, even teachers and examiners, actually believe that it is correct. It is not.

The aim of quality riding is to have a comfortable horse gently giving to, and mouthing his bit, and flexing comfortably from the poll. The horse *cannot* do this unless he opens his mouth slightly. Fastening a noseband so tightly that the horse cannot open his mouth (bottom right) is actively preventing him doing what good schooling is aiming for. Furthermore, a horse cannot breathe through his mouth, and a tight noseband often restricts the airflow through the nostrils, which is frightening for him.

The bit

Another appalling current fashion is to raise the bit so that it sits far too high in the mouth. This can cause pain to horses, seen in their faces and eyes. It also causes a dull, insensitive mouth by stretching and maybe splitting and callousing the corners of the lips, and preventing the bit acting correctly in the mouth (see above, lower photo).

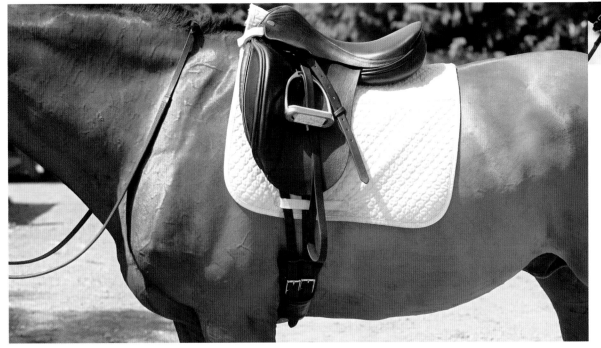

Fitting bits high like this is also confusing and upsetting to the horse because it gives a constant 'stop' or 'slow down' aid (due to the pressure of the tight adjustment), whilst the rider's legs and maybe spurs and whip are giving the horse 'go' commands, perhaps very strongly (and constantly, which is not effective) – because the horse is not, understandably, going freely forwards! This is clearly a crazy situation.

The saddle

Even if a saddle fits well, the way it is placed and adjusted makes a big difference to the horse's comfort and action, to the seat of the rider, and so the application of the aids. The main problem I find is that many people put the saddle on too far forwards (see top photo), so they are sitting almost on top of the withers and shoulders. The results of this are as follows:

• The saddle interferes with the movement of the tops of the horse's shoulder blades, and so with his ability and willingness to reach out freely in front. The shoulder blades extend from the points of

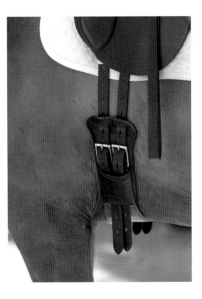

the shoulders to the withers, and in movement rotate around a point about a third of the way down the shoulder blade from the withers. If the saddle is too far forward, the tops of the shoulder blades will rotate back and come underneath the front part of the saddle, and suffer pressure, discouraging the horse from moving the shoulder and foreleg freely forward.

• This problem is exacerbated if the girth is too far forwards (see above, lower photo), and likely to dig into

the tissues behind the elbow.

• This positioning tilts the saddle up at the front (top photo), inclining the rider back towards the cantle, and concentrating their weight on the back of the saddle instead of spreading it evenly over the whole panel beneath the seat. The rider will be displaced and unbalanced.

• The stirrup bars are then too far forwards, and are also slightly tilted downwards. This pulls the rider's feet forwards, making it difficult for him/her to maintain a balanced seat with the ankles beneath the seat bones, and increases the likelihood of the leathers slipping off the bars.

• At every step with the forelegs, the saddle will be pushed up and over from side to side, rocking it on the horse's back and beneath the rider's seat, making it difficult for the rider to sit properly still.

To avoid all this, assuming good saddle fit and balance, place the saddle far enough back that you can fit the side of your hand between the top of the shoulder blade and the front edge of the saddle. If the saddle then comes too far back on the loins, it is too long for the horse's back.

Be prepared

15 Have a good trainer available

You may well be thinking: 'I thought this book was about improving my own schooling skills.' True, but a trainer who accords with your aims and principles is worth his or her weight in gold. We all encounter problems, and an outside eye can often help. Someone with a gift for training, teaching and *understanding horses* can take you further than you ever dreamed possible.

How can I find a trainer who shares my beliefs?

One of the best ways is to ask around all the horse owners that you know, and quiz them about the principles their teacher follows during lessons. The next step is to go and watch some lessons given by those teachers or trainers who sound as though they would agree with your beliefs.

Obviously, the next stage is that you approach them, even if only for a card, and either discuss matters there and then, or 'phone them later.

If you are interested in a particular discipline – be it eventing, dressage, classical riding, show jumping, or showing – you will probably find it easier to find a teacher because they should be known within their discipline locally, or they may be registered with a particular administrative organization.

Most teachers charge not only for their lesson time, but also for mileage (petrol, plus wear and tear on their car). A few also charge travelling time, but usually only if they have to travel quite some distance. This, and the matter of insurance, must all be sorted out. Some teachers only take clients who will travel to their yard, either taking their own horse or having a lesson on a horse belonging to the teacher.

Another way to find contacts is to look at the adverts in the 'Instruction' or 'Tuition' columns of regional equestrian publications. You are quite entitled to ring and ask if you might come and watch a lesson, but freelance teachers who teach on other people's premises may have to ask the owner of those premises, not to mention the person being taught, if they mind your coming to watch a lesson. Most, however, will be willing to have you there.

A point worth mentioning is that those teachers who use microphones and earphones for their riders may not be worth watching because you cannot hear what they are saying. You could get some idea of their principles by watching how the horse goes, but this is only half the story if you do not know what the instructions were in the first place.

16 Get the most from your lessons

Lessons from a good teacher are not cheap, although the actual fee may be governed by local conditions. Nevertheless, it is better by far to have lessons from a good and possibly more expensive teacher once a fortnight or month, than weekly from an instructor who is not so good, even if he/she charges less. The difference between a teacher and an instructor is not just a play on words.

What will the teacher expect?

Your teacher should make clear beforehand that the horse must be sound and healthy, that his feet, mouth and tack must be in good condition, and that you need to wear a hard hat that is up to the current safety standard, and possibly a body protector at least for jumping, otherwise his/her insurance will be negated. You should wear correct riding gear, though there is no need to 'dress up'.

The teacher will expect you to be more or less ready when she arrives, although she may want to see you tack up, and she may make suggestions about your tack.

She will expect you basically to do as she suggests, or to tell her why you don't want to. A good teacher does not teach for money alone, but also from the sincere desire to help. Even if what you hear is quite different from what you are used to, try to comply.

She will also expect to be told of any behavioural, health or other physical problems the horse has had, and of his background and your aims.

What can I expect, in my turn?

You should expect from your teacher that they are polite and honest – not flattering you to get more business – and they should show a genuine interest in you and your horse.

They should take time to assess the pair of you in all gaits (unless there is one you do not wish to tackle), and may, during this process, ask you to perform particular movements, or to alter your technique or riding position. If you cannot hear clearly, tell them.

There is a common belief that a teacher should be prepared to get on your horse, set him up, and/or demonstrate. Some do this, but I do not agree that it is essential. Conversely, some get on at the earliest opportunity, spend almost the whole time riding your horse, and end up teaching you very little. Some treat the lesson like a social occasion and, again, teach you little. Neither of the last two scenarios are any good to you.

You may know after one lesson that this person is, or is not, the teacher for you, or it may take a few lessons. Whatever your gut feeling, give them a fair chance to help you before making your final decision.

31

Groundwork

Training horses from the ground

Ideally, every horse would be trained from early foalhood to lead, move around, stand still, respond to voice commands, have his feet handled, wear a foal slip or little halter, maybe a foal rug depending on circumstances, and so on. Unfortunately it is increasingly common to come across poorly educated youngsters nowadays. Bad behaviour that is dangerous to humans and possibly other animals, even though it is perfectly natural to the horse, is often put down to the fact that a horse is 'only young' – but this does not excuse it.

When bad behaviour is found in older horses it is due to lack of education and training, and/or to ill-treatment or weak handling; these create insecurity and defensiveness, or over-assertiveness and even aggression. It is bad enough dealing with an ill-mannered youngster, but similar problems in a big, strong, mature horse can intimidate all but the best professional handlers.

What has this to do with training from the ground? Groundwork is the foundation for basic good manners, for respect for the handler, and later, for ridden or driven work. If you have a poor relationship with a horse on the ground, it won't improve just because you sit on him. Working from the ground gives you a chance to study closely your horse's facial expressions and body language. It also enables you to instil into him reliable co-operation with vocal commands, to get the horse completely used to all aspects of being handled, positioned in the stable and out, respectful of you and your personal space, fairly disciplined as he would be in a herd, wearing tack and rugs – indeed, everything that makes him a pleasure, and safe, to have around.

Only when your horse has reached this very basic level of education in manners and safety should you contemplate lungeing as a precursor to long-reining and backing or starting. This should be a natural progression from correct handling and ground training.

There are many groundwork systems to choose from now, from whatever is traditional in your country, to other systems devised, usually, by individual trainers, behavioural practitioners, and so on, all with slightly differing beliefs and methods. Some of the most well known (and best publicized) methods can result in nervous, frightened, confused horses, or in horses that look to me like zombies, going around in an almost brain-washed trance, and not calm and interested, which is what I want.

The end result of your groundwork should be a mentally confident, willing and reliably co-operative horse, and this is achieved by education, training and discipline, and not mental and physical bullying and cruelty. I have studied several systems, and with one exception, I always abandon them as a whole and revert to humane, common-sense classical groundwork and ridden techniques, although I may use certain ideas from individual trainers provided they are humane.

Most of us will have seen impressive displays of advanced training in horses at liberty, on the lunge and on long reins, displays that show how far you can take a horse's training without ever getting on him. Groundwork can be an end in itself, if that's what you want. As an introduction to ridden work, training from the ground cannot be beaten.

17 Teach your horse to stand still and stay

The most important thing from a safety and manners point of view is to teach your horse to stand still, and it is surprising how many don't. If a horse is standing still, including keeping his head reasonably still, he cannot do any harm. Obeying the command 'stand' is invaluable, whether from the saddle or on the ground, especially if you have fallen off or tripped up and are hauling yourself out of the mud.

The knock-on effect

It is surprising how co-operative and respectful horses become once they have learned infallibly to stand on command until they are told to do something else. It seems to colour their view of everything else, of humans and of life itself. Standing on command should be a horse's first ground rule, and it actually appears to give them confidence because it establishes their relationship with their handler.

How do I go about it?

Your horse must first be used to humans and to being handled firmly and fairly so that he is confident that

he won't be hurt. He should wear a headcollar, halter or nose chain confidently, and preferably be used to the word 'no' as a corrective. Polite leading in hand makes this job much easier, as you can have trained him to the words 'walk on' and 'stand'.

Lead him to the back of his stable (no food around as a distraction) and as you bring him to a halt with light backward tugs on his headcollar, say 'stand'. The *instant* he does so – not several seconds later – say 'good boy'. Keep the rope loose and stroke him. If he moves, say 'no' and replace him exactly where he was, then say 'stand', followed by 'good boy' only when he does.

When he does this well, wait till the next lesson to stand further and further away from him, still holding the rope. If he moves at all, immediately say 'no', replace him, say 'stand', then 'good boy' and so on as before. (If the horse is wearing a bridle, use the cheek-pieces to place and stand him, as at left.) The horse will soon catch on if you use the words consistently and immediately.

Progress to working without the leadrope, standing further and further away. Finally, get him to stand in his doorway and in the manège. He then ought to stand and stay anywhere. Once the command is thoroughly learnt, your horse should become reliable at standing under saddle, too.

Once this is thoroughly instilled in his mind, everything else will become much easier.

18 Teach your horse to lead politely

One of the most common in-hand problems is a horse who leads his owner, rather than the other way round. Nor is it helpful that very often teaching organizations instruct their students to position themselves level with the horse's shoulder when leading; this is just asking to get your feet trodden on should the horse skip to the side, and mentally it also gives the horse the upper hand. Here's a better way.

Leading equipment

Most problems occur with difficult horses who have been led in an ordinary headcollar and have been able to get away with bad behaviour (see above). A plain headcollar gives very little real control when you've got a stroppy horse on the end of the leadrope. There are various patterns of restrainer or controller headcollars and halters on the market that give more control *as long as* the owner is trained in their use – otherwise harm can be done to the horse.

Some people like to lead tricky horses in a Chifney anti-rear bit, but my experience is that this bit can actually encourage some horses to rear. Leading in a bridle on a public road or in any public place may now be required by insurance companies, but my favourite way of leading, which gives more control than a bridle and snaffle bit, is using a nose chain. Very few horses argue with these. The TTEAM chain and soft rope leads (*see* p. 116 and Useful Addresses) are also excellent. A good, strong, old-fashioned leather lungeing cavesson with a padded metal nosepiece is also fairly foolproof. Modern, softer nylon ones are nothing like as secure and effective.

What can I do?

A bit of technique and retraining is also helpful. It is safest, and gives you more control, to have your horse walk with his head level with your shoulder (see below). Whatever kind of headcollar you use, train him to back in hand. Hold the leadrope just down from the clip, face your horse and, keeping his head down, give quick, backward tugs on the rope, keeping it up till he backs, even half a step, then say 'good boy' immediately. A tap on the chest with a whip or a poke from your thumb reinforces the tugs, if needed.

When he will back to one or two tugs, teach him the word 'back' by saying it at the instant he steps back. Repeat this several times till he backs reliably, always praising promptly. Then have the lead fairly short to start, and walk level with his head. The instant he gets in front of you, say 'no', turn to face him, and back him a few steps, praise him, then lead again. Every time *without fail* that he gets in front of you, do this *immediately*, and he will soon lead with his head at your shoulder.

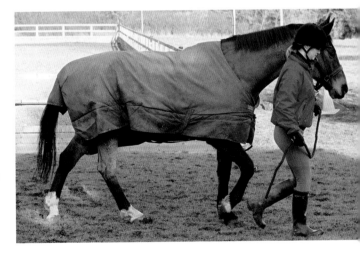

19 Teach your horse to lower his head

When a horse's head is low he is nearly always calm and relaxed. It is natural for horses to raise their heads when panicked, worried or frightened, and this is a preliminary reaction before they take flight, their inborn response to fear. If you can get the head down, you can often de-fuse a situation, either from on the ground (where you teach it first), or from the saddle, or when the horse is in harness. Try the following ways.

Method 1

Have your horse in a halter or headcollar with a leadrope. Hold the rope about 15cm (6in) from its fastening, and exert a firm, but not hard, straight-down pull on it. Rapid downward tugs can be used instead. The idea is that the horse has to work out and learn that pressure is removed when he moves his head away from it, so if he drops his head the pressure stops. This may take several seconds the first time. It is essential to keep up the pressure till you get the right response, otherwise the horse will learn that he can ignore it.

The important point for the trainer is to *not* lower the hand with the head when it goes down, as this will maintain the pressure and the horse will not experience the release, so learning nothing. You can repeat this a few seconds after his first successful attempt. Remember to say 'good boy' the instant he lowers his head. Once he lowers it readily, say 'head down' the instant the head goes down to get him to associate the command with the movement; repeat this and praise instantly as always. You should be able to achieve this from the saddle just on the command. If it does not happen, the horse is not sufficiently confirmed in the work in hand.

Method 2

Another way is to bend down and point to the ground, saying the horse's name (see left). As his head goes down, as it almost certainly will, say 'head down', then 'good boy'. Repeat this to get a reliable response in various places, and it should be learnt.

20 Teach your horse to come when called

This is something that hardly any horse does! At least, some come when they feel like it, but it is very rare that a horse will come when called like an obedient dog even when he doesn't want to. We are so used to this that we take it for granted that horses don't come when called – but well trained circus horses do, and so do some others, and if one can do it, they all can.

Why bother?

It's a real advantage to be able to call your horse to you when you want him to come in, instead of having to trudge out to get him, or worse, have him running all over the field playing difficult to catch.

And if you are out riding and you take a tumble, it's really helpful to have a horse who will ground tie – but if the reins don't fall over his head, he may not stop and wait. In such circumstances, knowing that he will come to call is a great relief.

What do I do?

Lead your horse on a long lead or half-length lunge rein, walking about 1.5m (2yd) away from him. Turn slightly towards your horse, and pull the lead firmly but gently to bring his head round to face you.

At this moment, use his name followed by a command such as 'here' or 'come', and walk backwards, holding your hands in front of your waist. Look him softly in the eye and walk more slowly than he is, so that he catches up with you. At this point, say 'good boy' and stroke his neck. Lead him around again and do the move about half-a-dozen times in different places around your yard, which should confirm the behaviour. Then repeat it all on the other rein.

If he doesn't walk towards you initially, be soft and submissive and give little, quick tugs on the leadrope, calling his name and your command, till he does, then say 'good boy'. And in order to teach him to come from a distance, it also helps to adopt the above body posture, so that he associates it with coming to you. When you go to the field, call his name to get his attention, fold your hands in front of you, say the command and walk backwards. The behaviour should become a habit with him.

21 Teach your horse to yield his hindquarters

We must all have ridden horses who only respond to a leg aid by moving forwards or faster. This can be most frustrating when you are trying to position them at a cross-roads, when opening a gate, or when moving around amongst other horses. Lack of manoeuvrability can be dangerous, so I like to teach sideways yielding quite early on in a horse's education.

Start right

A well mannered horse needs to be manoeuvrable on the ground and under saddle. This does not mean near-perfect full passes (rarely seen these days except as performed by some High School horses, and police and military horses), but sideways movement when and where asked. Start with the hindquarters to give you control of the 'engine', and lead on to ridden turns on or about the forehand. This also forms an initial lateral lesson and helps with stable manners.

To be 'correct' the horse should cross one hind leg under his belly in front of the other, then push away with it as the other leg moves outwards and the steps are repeated. Done to both sides, this causes development of the muscles down both sides of the horse's legs. The 'easy way out' is to move the outer leg to the side first, then simply bring the inner leg, which is supposed to cross in front of it, up to it but without crossing. This does move the hindquarters, but horses form habits very easily and so will readily adopt this less strenuous version unless corrected – and it is as well to insist on the correct way to do this, rather than simply to allow the wrong one, from the very start.

What do I do?

Stand your horse up wearing his headcollar, halter or bridle. Stand on, say, his left side level with his head. Hold his leadrope fairly short with your left hand to prevent him moving forwards, and have a long schooling whip in your right hand. Face his tail and, pulling his head slightly left towards you, lightly tap his left hock with the whip constantly and rhythmically till the horse just lifts the leg. *Immediately* stop the tapping and say 'good boy'.

The horse will soon cross the leg over the other one and move away. *As he is doing so*, say 'over', then 'good boy'. Instant praise is always needed for a good response. Eventually you can tap higher up on the thigh, and finally use a light hand touch on the ribcage where the rider's leg will ask for this from the saddle (say, under the cantle). Keep using 'over' from both sides so you can use the same command when you are actually riding him. Progress with repititions over a few days, keeping the head straight between attempts.

22 Teach your horse to yield his forehand

Moving the forehand is a follow-on to moving the hindquarters. In hand it has significant advantages (see below), and from the saddle it is important for suppling the horse, obtaining co-operation, and in movements such as opening gates and manoeuvring round obstacles or on tricky ground. It also accustoms the horse to bearing weight on his hindquarters.

The mental and physical benefits

The training for this is similar in principle to the previous topic. Moving a horse's forehand sideways can also be invaluable when dealing with a frightened, confused or stubborn horse who has rooted his forefeet to the spot and will not or cannot seem to move, such as when working under saddle, doing groundwork, being led around or loading into transport. Moving the forehand over, sometimes from one side to the other and back, seems to remove the block and get the feet moving again, as well as calming the horse down. In cases like this it is important to keep the head down to discourage fear and panic, and to encourage calm and relaxation.

What do I do?

Aiming to turn the forehand to the right, stand slightly to the left and in front of the horse's head, holding the leadrope fairly short, and face his tail. Have your whip in your right hand, pull his head away from you slightly to his right and tap the side of the left knee continuously and rhythmically till the horse lifts the leg. *Immediately* stop the tapping and say 'good boy'.

Repeat over a few days: each time you should get an improved response until the horse is crossing the left foreleg in front of the right. Whilst he is actually crossing and

moving away, do not tap; say 'over', then immediately 'good boy'. Eventually you can tap once with whip or finger on the forearm, and ultimately immediately behind the girth where the leg will give this aid from the saddle. Always use the same command, and praise instantly.

Again, train this from both sides. As with any new movement, it is good to ask for it in various different places and several times in each, so that the horse does not associate whatever movement it is with only one particular place in the school or field.

23 Teach your horse to stop

If you have ever led around or worked a horse in hand who just will not stop, you will know how frustrating it is, not to mention dangerous. And when he does this on the lunge, the whole process becomes damaging and pointless. It seems like bad manners on the surface, and can indeed be that, but more often it is lack of effective training by past or present handlers.

Preliminary thoughts on stopping

The handler who can cause his horse to stop infallibly has control not only of the horse's body but also his mind, because he – the handler – has created a habit. It's an almost automatic association. As in topic 17, when a horse is standing still he can't do any harm so it's a crucial safety move – or rather non-move.

How do I do it?

I like to do groundwork in a TTEAM (Tellington Touch Equine Awareness

Method) chain or zephyr lead, or improvise for instance an ordinary nose chain. With horses who do not stop you sometimes need something which, if required, will instil a little more respect than an ordinary headcollar. Restrainer or controller headcollars can be used if the handler knows how to use the particular type. I do not like to train such horses in a bridle because of the possible effect on the mouth; such horses often pull and do not respect a snaffle, anyway.

Do the early training in the stable to let the horse get the feel of whatever headgear you are using. If he is really reluctant to stop, start by walking him towards the wall or into

a corner and, as he reaches it, give a light, backward tug (not a sustained pull which makes things worse) on the leadrope. Do this until you can stop him short of the wall with a light tug. Then walk him away from the wall and tug, and so on. When he stops in the stable, take him to the manège, and practise in the same way there.

Once he is stopping to the feel of the tug on his nose, as soon as he begins to stop, say 'stand' so he comes to associate the action with the command. Always praise him the instant he stands. Soon he should stop promptly at a tug or the command.

24 Teach your horse to back easily

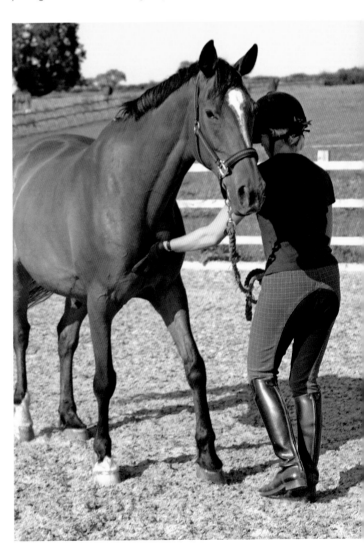

The first stage of teaching a horse to step back has been covered in topic 18 (see p. 35), but here we can go into it in a little more detail. Some behavioural trainers feel that making a horse back is a sign of psychological dominance on the part of the trainer, as you are 'forcing' the horse out of your personal space (even though you are following him!). Whatever the theory, however, stepping backwards is an essential movement for the horse to learn.

Why is it important for the horse to learn to back?

Backing (or reining back) is important for manoeuvrability and safety. A horse should back away immediately someone goes to enter his stable to allow them in, and should not stand barring their way or, even worse, try to push past them as the door is opened. The old rule of good manners was that the horse should go to the back of his box and stand to attention there until told to move, but few horses are taught to do that these days.

Ways of teaching a horse to back

The method of teaching the horse to respond to backward tugs on the leadrope has already been discussed.

Another method is to teach the horse to back by tapping with the whip on his chest (as on the legs for sideways movement). Simply stand in front of, and to one side of the head, facing the tail and holding the headcollar leadrope loosely. Continuously and rhythmically tap the chest with the whip. Do not put pressure on the leadrope. As soon as the horse makes to move backwards, stop tapping and say 'good boy'. After a few seconds, repeat the process and expect a full step back, stop tapping and praise. Then rest, repeat and expect two steps back, stop tapping and praise. About half a dozen little requests like this should confirm the behaviour. On another day do the same whilst standing at the other side of the horse.

When he is used to this, teach him the command 'back' by saying it *whilst he is backing* so that he associates the sound with the movement. This will eventually transfer to your being able to just say 'back', and he will do so.

If you watch horses together, you will see that when a horse wants another to get away from him he will pinch it sharply with his teeth as many times as necessary. This sharp on-off action seems to be naturally understood by horses brought up with others. To imitate it, we can use our thumb to poke, gently or more strongly, low down on the chest where the breastbone starts.

With a horse who already understands 'back', it may only be necessary to reinforce the command, if at all, by placing the flat of the hand gently on the breast.

25 Desensitize your horse to objects on the ground

Horses that shy and spook, nap, jib, plant themselves and generally make a huge fuss about objects on the ground are positively dangerous. Although it is natural for prey animals to be wary like this, when they are with humans it is dangerous and unwanted behaviour. If someone is on the ground near the horse they can be flattened, and if someone is on his back, the rider can have a nasty fall.

The fundamental problem

If a horse plays up regularly about (to us) everyday objects when ostensibly in the control of one particular person, the fact of the matter is that he does not have sufficient trust in that person to protect him, or respect for them so that he behaves safely when told to do so. These issues are down to the human to correct – most can be greatly improved, except possibly in the case of a horse having had a truly terrifying experience. Calm confidence is essential in the trainer, otherwise things will get worse.

Bombproof schoolmasters are not born that way, although horses have differing levels of the propensity to be highly strung or nervous, and so are likely to play up around objects which to them are suspicious. Also, some take longer to learn than others.

What can I do?

The basic method of desensitizing horses to 'monsters' is to subject them little by little to increasing levels of exposure. If you don't push out the boundaries the horse will not learn and improve. Before you start, your horse needs to be obedient to vocal commands, watching a whip for positioning and guidance, and to have good manners in hand in non-frightening situations.

From your viewpoint, it is safer to do this work on the ground because you can't have a fall, also the horse can see you and take heart from your presence. You need to wear a hard hat, gloves, strong boots and possibly a body protector. Have a schooling whip (I like my white TTEAM 'wand'). For the horse, use headgear of your choice, and be certain you know how to use it, but remember that a bridle is not good enough (not enough control and potential damage to the mouth) and neither is an ordinary headcollar. Use a long lead (about 4m/12ft) or a lungeing rein so that you have some play, and can stay out of the horse's way if things heat up. Also, this helps you keep hold of him: if he learns he can get away you have double the problem.

Using a reliable lead horse is fine at first, but your horse *must* fairly soon learn to pluck up his own courage.

Start in a familiar environment, walking between your horse and the 'monster' (a) to help him, and (b) so that if he shies away you won't get flattened. Have your whip in the hand away from the horse pointing forward to the ground to encourage the head down, a sign he should be familiar with. Walk calmly and confidently, with a loose lead, at a distance you know will not worry him, watching him all the time to gauge his movements; then approach a little closer, and so on till he shows a slight reaction.

Keep walking, say 'walk on' and push his head *away* from the monster. (An assistant some distance from his outside hip may help to discourage swinging away.) Praise him only when you are past it, then repeat till he shows no reaction. Then repeat on the other rein. Depending on how stressed out you or he are, try taking him fractionally closer, and so on, so that you make some significant progress; or if you feel you've made a major leap forwards (maybe literally!), try later in the day, or as soon as possible afterwards to get him to pass closer, and so on.

Try then, maybe on another occasion, to move the 'monster' somewhere else and repeat the process. This is essential so that the horse does not associate the 'cure' with only one place. It is most important that you keep at this technique and with different objects so that the horse develops a couldn't-care-less attitude. Only one or two tries is quite insufficient, even if the horse *appears* to become blasé, and may actually confirm the playing up behaviour.

26 Use obstacle courses to engage your horse's brain

As a 'follow-on' from the desensitizing process, or just as a good ploy on its own, creating obstacle courses for your horse is a marvellous way of getting him to concentrate on work, to pay attention to you and your signals or aids, to work things out for himself, and to treat a variety of items with aplomb. You can make them simple or complex, and later, can ride around them.

Isn't it enough just to school normally?

Possibly, but why not take advantage of every way you can think of to make your horse as well rounded, well educated and worldly wise as you can? Although in practice, brainwork does not use up so much energy as physical work, it does make horses tired – especially when they are not used to thinking! Well, of course, all horses think, but many horses' attention during ordinary familiar work is split between what the rider is asking, and what is going on nearby. Who knows, maybe they also think about what they'd rather be doing?

It is really interesting, and gratifying, to see how the attention span of horses taught this way increases, how their problem-solving abilities improve, and how quick they become at working out what to do and where to put their feet in difficult situations. They are also more prone to listening to and watching their 'person', and although you might think that this would suppress their initiative, in practice it enhances it.

What can I do?

Get together as many safe objects as you can find about the yard, and maybe buy a few others – feed buckets and tubs, traffic cones, flags and banners, matting or old carpet, sheets of strong plastic, jump stands minus the cups, plastic jump blocks, poles, balloons, old clothes and rugs, people with umbrellas or prams – almost anything the horse might meet, and that he needs to ignore.

Kit out yourself and the horse as in the previous topic, just in case, and make sure his shoes and feet are in good condition, with no loose clenches, protruding heels or broken horn to catch on obstacles such as matting.

Make it simple at first, and use items he is familiar with. If your horse is the flighty sort, put him through the desensitizing programme first. Start by, say, placing three upturned feed tubs of different colours spaced out in a

row, and take him into the field or school. Even the sight of something different alerts some horses as, to a horse, a change in the environment often means danger. Rugs don't belong on the ground in the school! Approach calmly and confidently, pointing the way with the whip, encouraging a head-down posture for relaxation and attention, and simply thread your way in and out of the tubs, praising him when he does well, and saying 'walk on' if he hesitates and 'good boy' when he passes it.

If there is anything he is a little suspicious of, take him back and stand by it for a minute or so, stroking him and calming him; but don't say 'good boy' till he ignores or passes it.

Then make things a little more difficult by adding different items and making a bigger shape such as a figure of eight that he has to walk around. If he has a 'spooky' corner of the school, make sure to put things to walk around or over in that corner, so as to distract him from his previous worry.

You can eventually make quite a complicated course, using everything you have. Combining items helps vary things: for instance, hang a rug on top of a jump stand, place traffic cones at each end of a mat to walk over, have people holding up a 'bridge' of plastic sheeting, tie balloons to feed tubs, and flags on to jump stands with poles or a tiny jump between them.

Use your imagination and set up courses in different parts of your premises until your horse just thinks you are completely mad but at least *he* is in control of himself!

45

27 Understand the benefits of lungeing

Where would we be without lungeing? How easy it is to lunge a horse instead of riding him when we're busy, or get the itch out of his heels before we ride him, or at a competition. Although everyone knows that lungeing is used during the backing and riding-away procedure, there can be so much more to it than that – and there are definite right and wrong ways to do it.

What is the basis of lungeing?

Horses have probably been trained on long ropes for thousands of years, but the modern concept of lungeing is mainly an old French one, '*longer*' being French, meaning 'to work a horse on a long rein'. Many people still call it 'longeing' rather than 'lungeing'.

Horses have to be accustomed to lungeing gear, and they must be taught to lunge. There are various methods, but the specifics of traditional lungeing are discussed more comprehensively in other books (see Further Reading p. 150), so I'll discuss different aspects of lungeing here, for interest.

The benefits of lungeing

Lungeing is a logical follow-on to work in hand, which should have accustomed a horse to obeying vocal commands and wearing equipment, also to the sight of a whip, the feel of it being stroked all over him, and the handler moving towards and away from him on a long lead, before lungeing proper is started.

Because there is no weight on the horse's back, the young horse, or one being rehabilitated, can find his balance and build up his strength more easily on a large circle or oval, which is a much more testing route than a straight line. A common and major mistake is to lunge horses on a circle that is too small (p. 47), which can damage their joints, their posture and their minds. Let the rein out and go with them (this page).

Lungeing enables the trainer

to accustom the horse to the idea of flexion, and of obeying the voice and the positions of body and whip when he is some way away; this instils the habit of co-operation and attention, and also enables the horse to develop his gaits and transitions, including jumping, more easily, since he has only his own body to think about.

Depending on your school of thought, various items of tack and equipment may, or may not, be worn by the horse to help (never force) him to adopt a beneficial posture (see topic 2). The trainer and horsewoman Sylvia Stanier is, at the time of writing, experimenting with using only one side-rein for lungeing – the outside one, because that is the master rein when riding – and is finding that some horses seem to go better in this way.

Finally, lungeing is the fore-runner to long-reining, with which you can achieve so much more.

The limitations of lungeing

One disadvantage of lungeing is that you cannot change rein as smoothly as when you are long-reining, because you have to go to the horse and change sides, then send him off again. (I prefer going to the horse, rather than bringing him in, as it can be difficult to keep a horse out and away once he has learned that coming in means a halt in the proceedings. Going to him is also, it is said, a dominating act, as you are invading his personal space and this helps him to see you as 'one who must be obeyed'. With a young or difficult horse this is helpful, although it is not so desirable with a horse with whom you already have a good partnership.)

You do not have as much control over your horse when you are lungeing as you do when you are long-reining.

One way of improving this situation is to use a strong but supple leather lungeing cavesson, with a metal noseband padded and covered with leather. (Fix your rein to the front ring.) The type with a throatlatch and a jaw strap stay in place very well and do not twist on the head like the softer, modern nylon ones, causing discomfort and lack of control. Horses rarely fight these traditional cavessons, yet they cannot hurt the horse. Only sensitive trainers who genuinely have good hands, equestrian tact, and who know what they are doing, should lunge from the bit.

Many horses learn the terrible habit of charging round in a circle on the lunge – although some 'trainers' actually encourage them to do this, mistaking speed for impulsion and extension. It is not easy to retrain a horse that has acquired this habit, and thinks he is doing what you want.

47

28 Understand the benefits of long-reining

Long-reining is so much more versatile than lungeing that I cannot understand why more people do not try it. It does not have to be complicated, and can make a real difference to a horse's outlook on life. It is not reserved for the world's classical academies, driving horses or 'natural horsemen'. Everyone and every horse and pony can benefit from it.

What is the basis of long-reining?

Long-reining seems to have come into its own just a few hundred years ago when Baroque equestrianism was a major and fashionable part of the education of royalty and the aristocracy. There are various methods of this skill, which are described in greater detail in other books (*see* Further Reading p. 150); two traditional methods are the Danish (very versatile) and the English.

The advantages of long-reining

In long-reining there are, of course, two reins, and the trainer can walk behind or at the side of the horse. The horse must be accustomed to the reins touching his back and hind legs (see below), and a sensible assistant is helpful in the early stages. She can calm and reassure the horse, and also lead him to help give him the idea (see p. 49, top photo).

The advantages for the horse are freedom from weight, as with lungeing, but also a more varied working pattern (it is easy to change from one rein to the other). From the trainer's viewpoint, you have more control than when lungeing. Long-reining can be used to exercise horses out and about (not just on their home grounds) because of the excellent control factor.

Long-reining can be a very fine art in equestrianism, and horses can be trained up to the highest levels of High School work, including classical airs on and above the ground, on long-reins.

They can also simply be given an excellent grounding in muscle-building, co-operation and using their initiative, as the trainer is not so visible and the horse goes ahead.

It is possible to school children's ponies to a high level of performance and obedience on long-reins. The ponies at the small, classically based riding school I attended from the age of four were schooled in this way.

The limitations of long-reining

Some behavioural practitioners maintain that long-reining dominates, even bullies horses, because it mimics the stallion's herding position behind his herd; however, I do not consider that horses feel this, and believe it is just one of those theories that doesn't work out in practice. (Of course, it is possible to bully a horse in any kind of work, but

bullying is not schooling – it is abuse or even torture.)

A disadvantage for the trainer is having to learn to use two reins plus a whip as a guide, but this is only the same as in riding. There is also the factor of needing to be fit and agile to get the best out of long-reining, but the work itself makes you so (see above).

From the horse's viewpoint, over-harsh use of the reins, or simply a handler with insensitive hands, can damage the horse's mouth and ruin his attitude. However, you can always use a good, traditional lungeing cavesson as described in the previous topic on lungeing, and you will achieve work of a high standard.

I believe that long-reining is a skill that is well worth learning for anyone who aspires to be a good horseman.

49

Flatwork

A plan for success

Correct flatwork is essential for any horse in order for him to be optimally developed, whatever his job. Being able to carry out basic flatwork exercises and carry himself in balance for his level of training is essential for a horse to be able to progress to greater things, and do them well without being forced in mind and body. It is always possible, by means of harsh methods, to get a horse to perform movements for which he is not sufficiently physically developed, or which he is not mentally able to understand as related to his normal work. This is not horsemanship, however, and produces only a travesty of the movement attempted.

Only a couple of human generations ago, unless a horse were schooled to what we now call Medium dressage level, he was not considered to be a made (fully schooled) riding horse, namely safe, pleasant and easy to ride in all normal circumstances. Note the word 'Medium', which is just that: a mid-level achievement, really nothing out of the ordinary.

Below is a proven progression of basic work that horse and rider need to master before going on to other things. Lateral work is integrated and dealt with in the next section. As a novice trainer, you should find this 'syllabus' very useful. The horse does not have to be perfect at each stage before moving to the next. Work consolidates as the brain adapts to absorbing that pattern of movement, and it becomes an established habit whilst the horse's mind is engaged on the next step. The horse does, though, need to be well balanced and co-operative at one level before progressing to the next.

Suggested progression

1 Walk on straight lines
2 Walk, showing slight inside flexion on shallow corners/large turns
3 Walk, showing slight inside flexion on 20m circles
4 Transitions from, and to, halt and trot without resistance (square halt not essential)
5 First three exercises in trot
6 Changes of rein with correct, slight flexions at walk, then trot
7 Transition from trot to canter in corner
8 Canter on straight line
9 Transition to trot from canter on straight line
10 Transition to trot from canter on 20m circle
11 Changes of rein (canter/trot/walk/trot/canter), *not* a formal simple change of rein
12 Changes of rein through trot
13 Improved, correct halts from walk
14 Circles down to 15m in walk
15 Circles down to 15m in trot
16 Rein-back without resistance, one step sufficient at first
17 Shortening and lengthening of stride (moderate) in all gaits
18 Improved transitions up and down, correct posture, without resistance
19 Circles down to 15m in canter
20 Walk to canter

29 Understand the influence of weight and focus

Your most important aid after your mind is your seat, and through it when necessary, your weight. Horses learn natural balance without a rider very early in life. They instinctively *want* to remain in balance so they can gallop more efficiently away from danger. I, too, and just as early in life, found that whichever way I leaned, my pony would go. I now know that it was because he wanted to stay in balance.

Balance on horseback

Think for a moment about the racing seat, on the flat or over jumps. The jockeys and work riders, particularly the flat-race ones, have very little leg to help them stay on. They do so almost entirely by balance, riding unschooled (by our standards), highly strung, nervous Thoroughbreds, often at speed, liable to throw themselves anywhere, at any time. This is a brilliant skill.

Observe the best flatwork and classical riders, and the more empathetic dressage and other riders, and you will see that they concentrate, knowingly or otherwise, on sitting upright. This sends their weight straight down to the horse's centre of balance a few inches behind his elbow about a third of the way up inside his chest from his breastbone. It moves very little when the horse is behaving normally, but when he is being naughty and perhaps throwing his body around, such riders can be seen trying to maintain an upright upper body position in order to encourage the horse to come back into balance (stop messing around) underneath them and to restore equilibrium.

Try this experiment

With or without a saddle and stirrups, walk your horse in a straight line with a *loose or free* rein towards some landmark you are thinking about and looking at unwaveringly. Be sure you are sitting centrally, and do nothing with your hands and legs; just sit still and relaxed, and concentrate on your landmark. Your horse will walk straight towards it.

Now set off on a straight line on your loose rein and aim to turn, say, to the right. You don't have to have a landmark, just think right and look ahead of yourself well round your intended curve. Do nothing with your hands, shoulders and legs, but *push your right seat bone forwards an inch or so.* Your horse will turn right. Repeat this to the left. Do it again, and this time put a little weight on your forward seat bone: your horse will make a tighter turn.

You can continue this game by riding two-, three- or four-loop serpentines, circles large and small, figures of eight – whatever it takes to convince you that your horse is obeying your seat and eyes (and mind). You can take up a little contact, take your stirrups back, but don't use your legs. The result will be the same, provided you don't interfere.

This basic position aid, or weight aid if you used weight, is the most natural aid you have to get your horse to go where you want him to. Of course, reins and legs can and will come into things and are very effective *if* used correctly – but your seat and weight are more important.

An imaginary case study

Being able to use your seat and weight subtly or more strongly is crucial to good schooling. Imagine you have a horse who habitually banks in in canter, say to the left. The worst thing you can do is to 'go with him' (lean left) because you feel you need to 'stay in balance' with him. This encourages the fault, because you are putting your weight where you in fact *don't* want him to go. Seventy-five per cent of your corrective action is keeping your upper body central and not leaning or tilting to right or left, to put your weight horizontally to the right, weighting your right seat bone and pressing on your right stirrup. For the rest, you can, simultaneously,

- carry both hands clearly and firmly to the right so that your left rein is pressing sideways on his neck just in front of the withers and your right is acting like an open rein (see next topic);
- keep your inside (left) leg like a supporting pillar down his side only just behind the girth;
- look and think out to the right.

By doing 'everything right' you've firmly and safely counteracted your horse's inclination and corrected his balance. I guarantee it works.

30 Understand the purposes of rein and leg aids

The earliest riders devised the means of making horses go and stop by using movements that came naturally to them: they kicked to make the horse go, and they pulled to stop him. A lot of people still do this today! However, the ancient Greek cavalry commander, Xenophon, already knew better 2,400 years ago, and he probably wasn't the first.

The leg aids

It's true that the legs basically mean 'go', or rather 'move away'. They also guide directionally, and reward or relieve by ceasing to act when the horse complies with their request or demand – *if* the rider knows his or her business. The main, and extremely common fault that many riders have, is to kick backwards with their legs, or rather raised heels. This is a beginner's trait, and sensitive, skilled horsemen do not do it.

The legs need to be used in specific positions:

• taken back from the hip (not just the knee) behind the girth, to activate, support, guide or control the hindquarters and hind legs;
• just behind the girth (that is, their normal 'hanging down' position) to create impulsion and forward movement;
• on the girth (in practice just on the back edge of the girth, although some use them more forward than this) to direct the forehand and forelegs.

They can be used in specific ways:

- by squeezing or pinching inwards;
- by being lifted slightly away from the side and tapping inwards to request forward movement if a nudge, squeeze or pinch doesn't work;
- by the heel being pushed down to increase tension in the whole leg, and create a strong aid (relieved by raising the heel slightly again);
- by brushing the calves from back to front for forward movement, or from front to back for rein-back.

The seat and legs should be dropped loosely, and not heavily, round the saddle and the ribcage. The legs should *not* be pressed constantly against the horse's sides, as this will deaden his response to the aids.

The leg aids can be backed up by a schooling whip (tapped or laid against the horse *only*) and spurs, preferably short, *rounded* ones. If the trainer cannot get a result with these and an appropriate voice aid, the initial groundwork training has been inadequate, the horse has not absorbed the 'forward' ethic, responding to a light touch, and you need to retrace your steps in his schooling.

The rein aids

There are different national schools of thought concerning the purpose and use of the reins, and different ways of expressing similar principles. The techniques explained (simply and basically) in this book are almost entirely the Iberian/old French techniques that I favour because they are reassuring and clear to the horse, and produce self-balance and lightness at all stages of training (in conjunction, of course, with the seat and legs).

The *outside rein* is the master rein:

- it regulates the horse's speed up or down, and his length of stride, by taking or giving;
- it yields to allow flexion away from it;
- it supports, often against the neck just in front of the withers, to steady, balance and guide the horse around turns and circles.

The *inside rein* is used:

- to 'talk' to the horse by means of little squeezes, tweaks and vibrations. It asks for longitudinal and lateral flexion of the poll and very top of the neck, and for relaxation of the lower jaw if the noseband is correctly adjusted loosely enough. Without these, correct posture in self-balance, and the resultant lightness in hand, are not possible;
- to ask the horse for a particular direction and way of going by being moved upwards or downwards, sideways (in or out), forwards and very rarely backwards.

An ideal, average contact for a relatively novice horse is a comfortable 'hand-holding' contact, consistent but flexible, on the outside rein, with the inside rein normally a little lighter. There is more on the subject of contact in topic 40 (see p. 70), and exactly what to do with seat, legs and reins is discussed in relation to individual topics and movements.

31 Warm yourself up

Just as you need to warm up your horse correctly before work, you, too, need to warm yourself up and limber up before mounting so that you are not at all stiff for the important and potentially dangerous job you are about to do – ride a horse. This loosens up your soft tissues and joints and gets the blood and energy flowing freely to them: in this state, your whole body works better.

Dismounted warm-up exercise

Although this may be more important in cold weather, it is a good idea in all weathers to do some sensible exercises that move the body and limbs smartly around in order to get the blood and energy circulating (although quartering and tacking up will achieve this); for instance, you could use arm and leg swings, and also leg stretches.

Start by loosening up your **head and neck**. Just roll your head around

fully both ways three times. In the first 'roll' don't go at all beyond your comfort point, the second time just push it a little, and the third time a bit more so that you feel that the tissues are being worked without being in the least uncomfortable.

Next, keeping your **arms** straight, swing them around on just the same principle, forwards and backwards in full circles three times.

With your **legs**, keep them and your back straight as you swing your legs forwards and backwards, holding on to something to keep your balance, if necessary. Three to five swings should loosen up your hips if you swing to the extent that you can reach easily, whilst at the same time feeling that you are almost at your limit. Because riders need open hip joints to enable them to spread their seat and thighs down around the saddle, next do about three sideways lifts to each side: standing with the balls of your feet on a step, relaxing your ankles and letting your weight drop down through your heels (*no* bouncing up and down) stretches the tissues down the backs of your legs and helps you to have a long, loose leg.

Mounted warm-up exercises

Roll your shoulders up, back and down and your ankles round and round both

ways a few times. Ride around with no stirrups and long, *loose* legs, toes hanging down, to get you well down in the saddle without heaviness. Riding without stirrups whilst pushing up your toes in fact stiffens your legs and adversely affects the sensitivity of your seat and position.

32 Communicate with visualization

Not so long ago, anyone who said that they 'thought' to their horse, and pictured to him what they wanted, would be considered half mad. Slightly less off-putting would be the notion that they imagined being a tree with roots stretching down and branches stretching up, to help their position – and similar. Nowadays, such ideas are quite accepted as being both helpful and effective.

How can horses possibly read our minds?

I don't know how, but I know that they do. This may be because I am equally certain that they read each other's minds and communicate to each other as much in this way as in any other, although there isn't space to delve into this here. So there is absolutely no reason why they should not try to communicate with us, and receive communications from us, as well as doing this with other horses or animals.

We have already discussed looking where you want to go as being an almost foolproof way of getting a horse to go there – and thinking it, with or without your eyes closed, also works. When I am teaching a horse and rider I know quite well, I often find that I will be about to ask the rider to do a certain thing and the horse does it before I say anything. The rider then corrects the horse, naturally enough, which must be a bit frustrating or confusing for him, but I can't think of a way round it.

How do you do it?

Simply by imagining or picturing in your mind what you want your horse to do, or how you want the pair of you to look and feel whilst doing a particular exercise. We have already mentioned the tree example to help improve your riding position; another is to imagine a squashy ball between your hips, to help with absorbing the horse's movement with your seat.

The technique is also very useful when dealing with difficult moments such as shies, spooks and so on. Simply picture hard to the horse that you are both riding past the monster, ignoring it, and this really helps to convince him that there is no danger. It works well when jumping, too, or loading into transport, and similar potentially stressful situations.

33 Warm up and cool down correctly

A horse needs to warm up properly *in all weathers* so that his tissues are better serviced by blood, lymph and energy, and are loosened up in preparation for the stresses that will be placed on them during work. This helps to avoid injuries to tight, stiff or cold tissues. Cooling down to help expel waste products produced during work is just as essential but is often disregarded.

So what's the best way to warm up?

It is essential to warm up on an absolutely loose rein, held on the buckle, to allow blood to flow easily through loose muscles. Control and safety are paramount, but give the horse as much rein as you dare, aiming to give him all of it as soon as he settles. Guide him with your eyes, body/weight, loose seat and legs.

A suggested routine Always encourage a horse to warm up with his head held comfortably low, but never behind the vertical. By 'holding' and supporting him with your mind, voice and whole body, keep him in horizontal balance (see below), going freely but not fast, with his back coming up, never on the forehand which can overstress the forelegs. *In time*, he will be able to perform the following routine in self-balance in trot and canter as well.

On your loose rein, walk one circuit of the school on your horse's best rein, then change the rein across the diagonal and do a circuit on the other rein. Next do a large figure-of-eight in two 20m circles and some big, loose serpentines. Do the same in a loose, flowing trot, still on a loose rein, and finally do the same in a loose, flowing canter (in half seat, slightly leaning forwards *from the hip joints, not the waist*), still on a loose rein. If the horse cannot do easy flying changes, come down to trot to change rein when cantering.

This routine can take ten or fifteen minutes, depending on the weather. It takes longer to warm a horse up in cold weather than when it is warm.

For many horses and riders, this will all be an achievement in itself, so you can be proud of the fact that your horse is now properly warmed up, listening, trusting you, and thinking 'free and forward' with the beginnings of a correct vertebral bow (see topic 2, p. 12) – an ideal start to the session.

And what's the best way to cool down?

Gradually, and again on an absolutely loose rein. During work, muscles have been working and there may be tiny muscle injuries. Nature's way of protecting these is to clamp up the tissues around them to prevent further movement. This can result in little knots of shortened tissues (muscle spasms)

which can be quite sore, and eventually can create an abnormal pull on the tendons. If left uncorrected they can get worse, so they need 'stretching out' as soon as possible.

Another reason for cooling down properly is to keep the blood flowing on for a while to help it really do its job of restoring worked tissues by supplying ample oxygen and nutrients. Just as important is its other job of carrying away the tissue debris and toxic waste products produced in higher amounts during work.

A suggested routine After any strenuous work (remember that schooling itself can be strenuous), keep your horse trotting on steadily, relaxed and on a loose rein, to keep the heart rate up a bit. After a few minutes, come down to a long-striding walk on a loose rein (see above) – at this point you may like to quit your stirrups

– and, after a few minutes more, slow the walk a little and ask the horse to walk in half circles small enough to necessitate his crossing the outside foreleg over the inside one as he turns (see right). Ask him to bend a little to the inside of each turn.

Change direction repeatedly so that he stretches the tissues down the whole of the outside of his body alternately. Finally, walk on both reins around the school, still on your loose rein and maybe with the girth loosened a hole.

Some people get a friend to loosen the noseband at this point, or jump off and loosen it and the girth themselves, leading the horse around for the final few minutes. If the horse then licks and moves his mouth around in relief, and there are marks to show where the noseband has been, it has been too tight.

59

34 Work in effectively, *then* do your planned work

Horses are schooled for four reasons: to make them safe and co-operative, to develop them physically so they can effectively and safely work under weight, to consolidate work already done, and to teach them new work. Along with all this goes the mental learning involved in any interaction with another creature, whether of the same or a different species.

What is working in?

After warming up (dealt with in the previous topic), it is safe to start asking the body to do some strengthening and suppling work, and to adopt a good weight-carrying posture with 'both ends down and the middle up' (*see* topic 2, p. 12).

Your horse needs now to start flexing his hindquarters under him at the lumbo-sacral joint (point of croup), bringing his hind legs under more and raising his back. Depending on his stage of training, he also needs to push his head and neck forwards in a long,

low arch, or push them more up (from the base of the neck) and forwards with the head flexed longitudinally at the poll. In no case should the front line of the face come behind the vertical (see above). This vertebral bow posture is achieved by riding 'from back to front' (see next topic).

The kind of work the horse needs to do for strengthening and suppling (loosening) should be in accordance with his capabilities, and *always in the correct, self-held posture* for his level of schooling:

- shortening and lengthening of the stride within the gaits;

- transitions to and from one gait to another, including halt;
- whatever lateral work he is capable of, such as turns on or about the forehand and haunches, shoulder-in (see right), shoulder-out and leg-yield;
- work over poles and maybe little jumps.

This is basic, routine gymnastic work for the horse, which both works and stretches his muscles alternately and promotes athleticism.

The horse only needs to perform the above movements once or twice on each rein for the physical benefits to occur; to drill him repeatedly will be destructive of his willingness to work and comply with your demands.

Your planned work

Opinions vary as to how often you should school a horse in a manège. Some say new work needs to be repeated a little every day for it to 'sink in', others maintain that two or three 15-minute sessions per week learning new work are enough. I agree with the second opinion: as you can do good work out hacking, if necessary, interspersed with looking around and experiencing different things out and about, it is good to vary your horse's work and environment. The whole point of schooling is to make the horse a reliable riding horse.

Obviously the specifics of the

schooling work you ask of the horse depend on what you are currently teaching him. After warming up and working in, spend around 15 minutes teaching your horse systematically, calmly and positively the next movements and exercises in his progression. Remember the four Ps:

- **Position** him so that he can actually perform the movement;
- give him the aid and let him **Perform** it;
- **Praise** him for the tiniest success;
- **rePeat** once.

Do *not* keep giving the actual aid whilst he is performing satisfactorily (he's already doing it, after all), but retain your correct body position to keep him in the movement. Be patient and happy with tiny amounts of progress, and do not push him beyond what he can give. Praise him instantly when he gives you even a hint of getting it right. Do the same on the other rein.

Give your horse plenty of breaks on a completely loose rein, walking or even just standing still with his head down. Finally, start your cool-down.

35 Ride 'from back to front'

The main purposes of the horse's forelegs are to bear the weight of the front of the body, and to accept and distribute the force of the energy coming along the spine from the hind legs and hindquarters. The main purpose of the hind legs and hindquarters is to propel the horse forwards, weight-bearing being secondary to this. The horse is a rear-wheel-drive animal.

What's the significance of that?

If the horse's power comes from behind, this means that, in schooling and riding, we need to concentrate on developing and allowing the effectiveness – the weight-carrying ability and thrust – of the hindquarters

and legs. Good methods of riding are based on enhancing the natural principles of equine biomechanics and the vertebral bow described in topic 2 (see p. 12). These are always the least damaging to the horse's physique; indeed they are beneficial to it, increasing its strength, power and agility, and, to our eyes, its beauty.

In such methods, the energy

produced by the hindquarters flexing/tilting under, and the hind legs thrusting the body forwards from well underneath the horse (known as 'engagement' – see above), passes along the spine and is received into the forehand, including the head and neck. According to the level of training, the head and neck will be stretched forwards, long and low or higher and

more arched, with the front of the face in front of an imaginary vertical line, or maybe on that line when in collection, depending on the horse's conformation. *If the horse is not tactfully taught and allowed to carry his head and neck appropriately himself, his back cannot rise and he cannot go as required.*

If the horse is going with a well developed vertebral bow (*see* topic 2, p. 12), in self-balance and with a voluntarily well carried neck and head, either going on the weight of the rein if sufficiently advanced or on a guiding but giving contact, he will reach out easily in front and spring along with flow and freedom, comfortably and willingly. His back and trunk will swing from side to side like a barrel on a rope, his tail will swing as well, he will over-track in walk, track up in trot, and have an easy, three-beat canter (not disunited or showing four beats).

What are the signs of bad schooling and riding?

Horses badly schooled and ridden show varied signs of distress, such as sweating, grunting, teeth-grinding, champing at the bit (if the noseband permits), laboured breathing, wide, frightened eyes, flaring nostrils, not accepting the bit, excessive frothing and drooling at the mouth and physical difficulty in going as the rider demands.

Any style of riding that produces any of these signs of distress in the horse is, in my view, cruel. Also, any style of riding that forces the horse to go in a way that is clearly uncomfortable (at the least) to him, and against the proven principles of good horsemanship, is damaging to mind and body. Points betraying such styles include:

- a forced and distorted outline, frame or shape that is clearly stressful for the horse to maintain;
- the neck being stiffly raised, shortened and often kinked downwards in front of the withers;
- the muzzle being pulled backwards and in, often with the front line of the face behind, and sometimes well behind, the vertical;
- or, conversely in some styles, the head being held up and out with the front of the face almost horizontal to the ground;
- the head and neck being held restrictively and rigidly in place, rather than clearly being voluntarily carried by the horse on a giving contact;
- lack of side-to-side swing in the back and tail, the body still and rigid, and the tail stiffly held or, worse, thrashing, with the horse usually moving from the stifles and elbows rather than the hips and shoulders;
- badly adjusted tack (a high bit and a tight noseband);
- back down and hind legs trailing;
- the horse having to be constantly driven or spurred forwards, but appearing afraid or unable to comply.

Such horses are not being ridden from back to front but from front to back. This is bad riding and schooling on whatever occasion you see it and cannot be called horsemanship.

36 Allow your horse to stretch right down frequently

One of the things I find it most difficult to do as a teacher is persuade riders, even in halt, to let their horses go completely free and stretch their muzzles right down to the ground. Most reins sold with ready-made bridles these days need extending to allow this, even though marked 'full size'; also, most riders have never been taught just how important stretching down is.

Why is stretching down so important?

When a horse works, his muscles spend a lot of time in a contracted (shortened) state because this is how they create movement. How muscles work, basically, and how a riding horse should hold himself (his posture) were explained in topic 2 (*see* p. 12), so we'll consider other, closely connected matters here.

A little test will help in understanding the different states of muscle tissue. Put your right arm out, palm upwards, and put your left hand on the right biceps muscle. Now raise your right forearm from the elbow joint and feel the muscle shortening underneath your hand. If you poke it with your fingers you will find that it is moderately hard. Do the same whilst holding something heavy or pulling against something difficult to move, and feel how much more tense the muscle tissue is. Finally, let your right arm drop relaxed at your side and notice how soft the muscle is.

If you could find a 'muscle-bound' weight-lifter or someone who works out incorrectly (all work and no stretching), you would notice that, even when in supposed relaxation, their muscles are fairly hard. Muscle-bound horses and athletes both have the same problem – their muscles are more prone to injury because they are

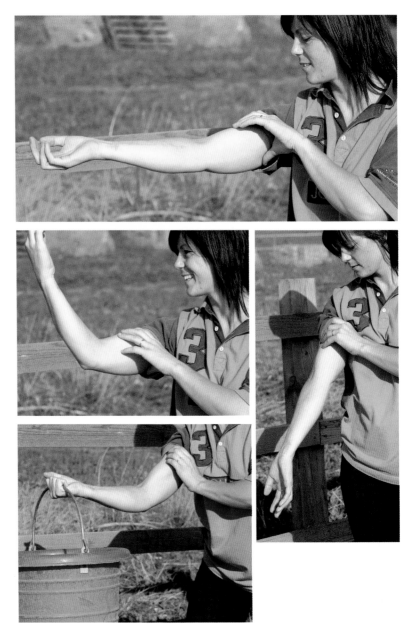

not stretched or relaxed enough during a working or schooling session.

Holding a muscle in a contracted state for many minutes at a time (I have seen it done for 40 minutes by a national dressage trainer) results in 'tight' tissue and possibly the little muscle spasms explained in topic 2 (p. 12). Standing stabled horses in restrictive contraptions has a similar effect, not to mention the obvious pain caused by both techniques. In its usual state, muscle tissue needs to be soft and loose to enable blood and lymph to pass freely through it and maintain its integrity and optimal functioning.

If a horse is allowed to relax frequently during work and encouraged to really stretch his head and neck right down with no restrictions – *or expected restrictions* from a rider who won't leave the reins alone, or from reins that are too short – blood and lymph

will flow freely through his tissues, and the muscles will never become semi-permanently tense and hard.

Stretching down not only helps the neck and shoulder muscles and tissues, but the whole horse, including the hard-working back and hindquarters (see above).

How can I put this into action?

Firstly you need reins long enough to permit it. Horses are very sensitive to any contact on the rein and may not stretch down if they feel there will be even a slight restriction on their mouths. Even leaving too-short reins resting on the withers will discourage the horse because he can sense the potential restriction. When you are sitting upright in the saddle with your elbows on your hips and holding the

buckle of your reins, the horse should be able to touch the ground freely with his muzzle on a still-loose rein.

During work of any kind, do not keep your horse in hand working up to his bridle for more than a very few minutes, say five at the most for a reasonably schooled, fairly fit horse, without allowing him the freedom to relax and stretch. When standing talking to your trainer, put the buckle on the horse's withers and ask him to stretch fully by saying 'head down' (see topic 19, p. 36) and praise him instantly when he does so. Allow him a couple of minutes like this, either standing still or walking around if it is a cold day, and make a habit of it.

Then you will have a horse who is physically in better shape and condition, and much calmer and more willing than most, because he feels more confident and comfortable.

65

37 Understand head and body flexions

Flatwork

Not many good riders are happy for their horse to go like a plank with little flexibility in his body or in his poll and jaw. Although it is stressed to us now that the horse has little natural ability to bend laterally in the spine, his longitudinal (up and down) flexion is slight but present, and his neck and jaw are the most flexible parts of his body. How does all this affect schooling?

What is bend?

All of us must have been told countless times to ask our horse to 'bend round your inside leg'. We talk about 'correct bend' (who says it's 'correct'? Not the horse!) and 'flexion at the poll' laterally and longitudinally. No one ever says, though, 'get him to flex at the croup joint' or, even less likely, 'ask for a flexion of the jaw joint'.

To ask a horse to flex at the croup (the lumbo-sacral joint between the lumbar vertebrae and the sacrum), we are usually told that we should 'get his hind legs under him' (as if they were somewhere else); and to ask him for a flexion of the lower jaw joint (the temporomandibular joint between the lower jaw and the skull, just below the

66

ear) we are told to ask him to 'give' or 'flex' to the bit. At least, we were 'in the old days'. No one seems to ask for, or be asked for, this flexion today, which is essential if the horse is to be free to softly accept and slightly play with the bit. This is probably because the current fashion is to strap the jaws shut with the noseband – so he can't flex the jaw joint anyway.

Why is 'bend' and the flexion of the joints in general so important to good riding? Because if your horse is not flexible in this way, he *will* go, and feel, like a plank: this is uncomfortable for the rider, it isn't an efficient way to move under weight, nor is it a strong posture in which to carry it.

Once horses have learnt that adopting and maintaining the vertebral bow (*see* topic 2, p. 12) is the most comfortable way of carrying weight, they are easy to place in this posture and usually adopt it voluntarily. If their heads and necks are restricted, though, or forced into 'an outline', and/or if their jaw joints are prevented from flexing (slightly opening the mouth by 'dropping' the lower jaw), it is impossible for them to achieve an effective vertebral bow because 'blockages' like this in any part of the skeleton (and pain and discomfort in soft tissues) affect the whole body and way of going.

Flexions at liberty If you watch horses playing and cavorting around at liberty, you soon realize that they have no conception of 'correct bend'; particularly when moving fast on turns, they usually go with their heads to the outside of the bend. If they didn't, they would fall over because there would be too much weight (the weight of the head) to the inside. The body usually leans in, and the inside shoulder leads – exactly what we try to 'correct' when riding!

Some probably Baroque riding master decided that it was much more beautiful to *our* eyes for horses to bend in the direction in which they were going, so we still do this today.

How does the horse flex or bend?

It seems that horses appear to bend round our inside legs mainly by carrying their ribcages to the outside and bringing their inside hips forwards (as we put our outside leg on behind the girth). We ask for inside flexion of the head and neck, so that we can just see the horse's inside eye and nostril (see far left photo, p. 66), and this makes a 'flexing to the circle' picture (see left). The following is a short résumé of how a horse flexes:

- The vital lumbo-sacral joint at the croup is 'flexed' by opening it and tucking the 'bottom' (the pelvis) under the body. The hind legs are attached to the pelvis so they, too, must come under the body, all of which engages the hindquarters.
- The poll flexes longitudinally at the atlanto-occipital joint between the atlas (the first vertebra of the neck) and the back of the skull. It is known as the 'yes' joint because it allows the horse to nod his head.
- The poll flexes laterally at the atlantoaxial joint between the atlas and the next vertebra, the axis. This is known as the 'no' joint as it allows the head to move from side to side without noticeably moving the neck.
- The horse 'gives' or 'flexes' to the bit by dropping his lower jaw to open his mouth slightly; this is done by opening the temporomandibular joint between the lower jaw and the skull, just below the ear.
- The vertebral bow is achieved by an upward flexion of the spine via the joints between the vertebrae.

You can see how important flexions are, and how damaging is any harsh style of riding which prevents them, damaging the horse's physique and his ability to go safely, comfortably and, for a ridden horse, correctly.

67

38 Sit classically – it really works!

'Classical riding is all about passage and piaffe and really advanced stuff, isn't it?' No, it isn't. It is about an extremely effective and humane system of riding from beginner levels upwards. The author was taught to ride classically from the age of four! The classical seat is said to be the basis of the best equitation systems in the Western world, but sometimes people get it wrong in practice.

The importance of seat and position

I know that many people don't want to be told how to sit and how to use their bodies – they just want their horses to improve. But they need to understand that if the rider isn't right, the horse will never be. Sitting correctly is all about weight control and effective aids, and you won't get either of these if your position and posture are a mess.

The standard seat

The following description should be familiar to most people who read their equitation textbooks for exams or for self-improvement:

The rider should sit on her seat bones (the bottom of the pelvis), not her buttocks, in the deepest part of the saddle, which should be midway between pommel and cantle for flatwork. The body should be held erect above the waist and the seat and legs

should drop, relaxed, round the saddle and the horse's ribcage, the stirrups taking the weight of the legs on the balls (widest part) of the feet. The rider should look ahead with the back of her neck pressed gently back into her collar, shoulders back and down and chest slightly raised. The upper arms should drop vertically down so that the elbows are *at the hips*. The seat bones should be pushed slightly forwards, 'tucking the bottom under' slightly and *not* hollowing the back. The ankle bones, or at least the heels, should be directly under the seat bones. Viewed from the side, an onlooker should be able to drop a straight, vertical line from the ear, through the shoulder, the elbow/hip and ankle, or down the back of the heel.

The advantages of this seat in practice

The muscles of the seat and legs being loose and still, not pressing down in the saddle or against the sides, favours a deep and secure but *not* heavy seat, so the horse is not discouraged from raising his back. This light, secure and still relaxation of seat and legs reassures and calms the horse: he is also sure that when you do use your seat or leg muscles you are actually giving an instruction, so there should be no confusion, and lightness reigns!

The seat and legs are the foundation of the seat and of all good riding.

(*See* topic no. 40, p. 70, for a further discussion of contact.)

39 Ride without stirrups

Riding without stirrups has long been a fundamental way to teach riders to acquire a deep, feeling and independent seat, and reliable, secure balance in the saddle. Like most techniques, there are right and wrong ways of doing it, and right and wrong horses on whom to learn it. The wrong technique and the wrong horse can wreck your style and shatter your nerve.

The horse for the job

You need a reliable, obedient lunge horse with very smooth paces who will go round steadily like clockwork. A horse who plays about, goes fast or 'banks in' to any serious degree can shatter your confidence and will do nothing for your skills.

A sympathetic teacher is a help, but a sensible friend doing the lungeing will do fine.

What should I do?

You are aiming to acquire a balanced seat that really goes with your horse, deep without being heavy, loose without being floppy. You can achieve this by the following means:

• Sit in the centre of a really comfortable saddle (using a seat cover of fleece or foam, if it helps) in the classical seat (topic 38) but without stirrups, and let your legs hang down completely loose with your toes dropping down.

There must be no tension at all in your seat or leg muscles. Any tightness will make you stiff and liable to be bounced around, whereas you need to mould around the horse.

• If you are holding the reins, do so at the buckle so that you are not tempted to use them to stay on. If you need support, hold the pommel or a neck strap. Sit upright and ideally lean back slightly, 'Red Indian' style. You must look ahead, not at the horse. In this way, you can sense his every movement.

• Set off in walk, staying loose in the lower body. When you are ready, ask for the horse to trot slowly. Lean back a little and drop your seat and legs around the horse as if you had no use in them, letting the horse move your seat from left to right as his left and right hind legs, respectively, come forward and his back dips on each side, but keeping your shoulders very still.

• Try the same seat in canter – shoulders back, down and still, raised chest, leaning back a little with loose seat and legs and inside seat bone forward a little. This is extremely comfortable and you will soon find your seat improving.

40 Understand nuances of contact

Contact is probably one of the most abused concepts in equestrianism. The point of having contact with the horse's head or mouth is, of course, control – getting through to the horse what you want, usually to stop, slow down or change his posture or way of going. Contact should be regarded as a back-up to your seat; however, many riders wrongly regard it as the Number One aid.

What is the ideal amount of contact?

The ideal contact is as little as you need to have the horse going in self-balance or self-carriage, and in correct posture for the gait being performed and the level of work. A well schooled riding horse should not burden himself or his rider by taking a really heavy contact, and vice versa.

- In the earlier stages of schooling, a guide to the contact of the outside rein (the master rein, remember) would be a reliably gentle, still but firm, 'hand-holding' contact, the sort you would use to guide a well behaved toddler across a road or to hold a bird in your hand without hurting it. This is steady and consistent but flexible, to support the horse.
- The contact on the inside rein can be more variable and lighter; this gives the horse a valuable sense of freedom whilst he still feels the control and guidance of his outside rein. This rein should be pulsed and 'felt' fairly firmly, then released, in a spongeing, give-and-take contact, to ask the horse to give to the bit, flex at the poll, and start to bring his back up and to balance within himself. When he does give, stop the rein aid, reapplying it only when he flattens and pokes his nose again. Together with forward aids from the legs (not at the same moment as the rein aids), this technique will develop a good way of going.
- When the horse 'engages' and also lightens in your hand, *do not take back the previous, firmer contact, because he has given you what you asked for.* The whole point is eventually to have the horse going in a correct posture and self-balance on no more than the weight of the rein. The weight of the rein does not mean *no* contact: it means a feather-light contact to which the horse instantly responds.
- To be truly sensitive to contact, a rider needs hands that are independent of the body, and this in turn depends on her having an independent, secure and balanced seat. Good riders never use the reins to support their seat, except in a real emergency. If your hands are helping to keep you on, or in position, they cannot possibly give sufficiently accurate and subtle aids. This will tell in the horse's mouth, and spoil his way of going.

41 Never nag with hands or legs

Many riders today use their hands and legs constantly, often at every stride. New clients often tell me they have been taught to do this because 'you have to be doing something every stride to keep on top of your horse'. This is rubbish. No wonder there are so many dull horses with insensitive sides and heavy mouths, who go far too fast but with no impulsion.

But my horse will stop if I stop kicking

Well, try it this way: think back to absolute basics – legs mean go, reins mean slow down or stop. Sit properly, keep your hands still, and get your horse going forwards. *As soon as* he is doing so, say 'good boy' and keep your legs still as well – no kicking, no jiggling on the reins, and no bouncing up and down with your upper body to keep him going. (The upper body does not create energy or movement anyway; only the seat and legs do that.)

When he slows down, *instantly* apply your legs (tap, pinch or squeeze inwards and forwards, not backwards)

with intention (as though you mean it!) and say 'walk on', which he should understand. Again, the very moment he speeds up in walk, *stop* the leg aid and say 'good boy'. Work on this, with crisp, spot-on timing, until your horse walks forwards instantly, and keeps walking on whilst you sit still and enjoy it, not slowing or stopping until you ask him. Some horses are slower learners, so be prepared for more repetitions and lessons with them.

Make your hands mean something

Just as constantly nagging legs make a horse switch off, so do constantly pulling or jiggling hands. How can

the horse pick out definite messages among all the chatter?

Read topics 30 and 40 (pp. 54 and 70), and keep your hands still and purposeful. Keep an appropriate contact on a still but flexible outside rein, but also use it for slowing, and for turning away from it when needed by pressing it intermittently sideways against the neck just in front of the withers. As for the inside rein, keep the contact light and still when you don't need to 'say' anything, and squeeze it intermittently when you need to ask the horse to give to the bit. As soon as he does, say 'good boy' and stop the aid. Good horsemanship demands a still, sensitive, secure rider who only does as much as necessary.

71

42 Understand 'Calm, Forward and Straight'

This is probably the most famous saying in riding. It was coined by General l'Hotte, a great French nineteenth-century classical rider and teacher. If everyone lived by it and practised it, riding in general would be very much better, there would be fewer confused riders, and most importantly, fewer confused, spoilt horses. But what exactly does it mean?

Calm

Briefly, if your horse is not calm, he will not learn anything good but could learn a great many bad things and have many unhappy associations. Excited, frightened, anxious, nervous horses can concentrate only on their emotions and maybe on what is causing them, if they know – but certainly not on their lessons.

To help keep a horse calmer, cut cereals right down or out and feed a fibre-based diet, maybe with soaked sugar-beet pulp and oil for energy. Give the horse plenty of time turned out with friends, and if there is no turnout at your yard, try to arrange some elsewhere.

Forwards

To have a horse 'going forwards' means to have him ready to instantly obey your seat and/or leg aids, even if they are asking him to go backwards. Impulsion goes with forwardness: it means controlled thrust, which is produced by the legs and easily controlled and distributed by the hands. Many horses go fast, but this is not the same as going forwards with impulsion.

Many people inadvertently stop their horse by having too heavy and rigid a contact, and because mentally they are afraid of his going forwards. Look up and forwards, and loosen the inside rein – then just enjoy it.

Straight

If a horse is not straight, with his hind feet following exactly in the tracks of his fore feet whether on a straight or a curved line (except in lateral work), his gaits and movements will not be 'true', the energy produced will not be correctly distributed through his body, and he will not be optimally developing the correct muscles for riding.

To instil straightness, imagine a railway track on the ground in whatever pattern you are riding, and put your seat bones on the tracks, then follow them. Ride also within 'the corridor of the aids', another classic classical concept.

Imagine that you are riding down a narrow straight or curved corridor in whatever pattern you want. The walls are your legs and reins; when the horse deviates, the wall pushes him back again.

Add rhythm and balance

I like to add 'rhythm' and 'balance' between 'forward' and 'straight'. Get a metronomic rhythm of your horse's gaits into your head, and keep it there in your mind, whatever the horse does. Once the horse has rhythm, balance will develop with correct, sensitive riding.

43 Understand the manège

There is no doubt that a good manège with markers and a sound surface is a godsend. It creates a sense of concentration and formality when schooling, and acts as a guide to accurate movements. It has been formulated over many years by skilled and experienced trainers and riders. Manèges can be any shape or size, but here we'll consider the standard one.

What does the word 'manège' mean?

Manège is French and means an 'arena for training animals'. It is often confused with 'ménage', meaning a collection of animals (hence 'menagerie') or a domestic household, and is used incorrectly.

How can I remember the letters on the markers?

Imagine you are riding in a standard dressage arena-size manège (measuring 20 x 40m): you enter at A, in the middle of one short (20m) side; you ride up the centre line, and at the top there is 'C', in the middle of the other short side; here you turn left, and you will see on the first long (40m) side H, E (in the middle) and K; if you turn right at 'C', to the next long side, you meet M, B (in the middle) and F.

To remember these, people have various sayings: a teacher of mine used to say, from 'A' clockwise: '**A**ll **K**ing **E**dward's **H**orses **C**an **M**ove **B******* **F**ast'!

K, H, M and F are each 6m up the long side from the corner. Exactly in between K and F is the notional letter D, exactly between E and B is X and exactly between H and M is G. D, X and G are exactly aligned with A and C. You can remember D, X and G by thinking of DOG, O replacing X.

What about tracks and quarter lines and so on? The route right next to the fence all round the manège is called 'the outside track'. A metre in from this is 'the inside track'. Five metres in from the outside track on the KEH side is 'the quarter line', and 5m in from the outside track on the MBF side is sometimes called the 'three-quarter line'. The short sides don't officially have quarter lines, but you can invent them for convenience, if you wish.

The route along ADXGC, or vice versa, is 'the centre line'.

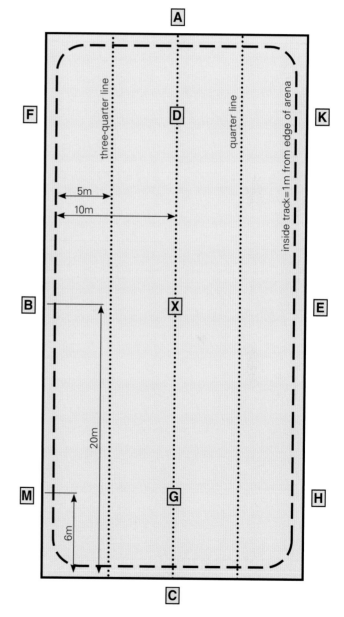

44 Ride in a straight line

Flatwork

To do this is not as easy as it sounds, but it is crucial if you want to compete in dressage competitions or simply have an athletic, co-operative and agile horse. How many times have you gone into a freshly raked manège, walked around the outside track, and then turned down the arena at C and ridden to A – and on looking back over your shoulder to see your beautiful straight line, are horrified by the wiggles and wobbles you have made!

Why are straight lines so difficult?

If you ever watch horses meandering around in their field, they almost never walk in a straight line unless they are deliberately making for a certain point, such as the water trough. Even then, you can see deviations and bends.

Horses, like humans, are not symmetrical from side to side, so they may wander a bit, not least because this is how they balance their bodies and stay upright. We're just the same. It's harder to do a straight line in walk than any other gait, next most difficult is canter (see right), and the easiest is trot.

How can I succeed?

Try riding straight lines across the school first, from marker to marker, or at least have a tree, post, or something else to fix your eyes on. Remember the railway track trick and the corridor of the aids (both in topic 42, p. 72). Have your horse nicely and comfortably in hand in a working trot, sitting with loose seat and legs. Turn across on to your straight railway track and inside your narrow corridor, and *look up at your marker, not down at your horse.* Ride in a businesslike manner towards it, and then turn away on to the track. Look back at your line and I'll bet it's really straight.

Next try a line down one of the quarter/three-quarter lines, then the centre line. Do the same in canter and finally in walk. The things to remember are to direct your horse with your seat bones along the railway track, control him within the corridor, and mentally tell him where you are going by looking at your marker. It never fails.

45 Ride a perfect 20m circle

This is another exercise that sounds simple but which is often done badly. So many horses and riders ride potatoes instead of circles, then look at the teacher in surprise when she asks them what went wrong! Horses tend to drift to the outside in the slower gaits because wandering is easier than circling, and they often bank in in canter, with their head to the outside, because this is how they balance in nature.

The place of circles in schooling

Twenty-metre circles are a basic test of a horse's acceptance of the aids and of his balance, and they will improve bodily co-ordination and his understanding of flexion and the aids. He has gone beyond the go–stop stage.

What's the best way to do it?

Imagine a circle to the right in walk:

- Your inside seat bone is pushed slightly forwards, which alone should turn the horse, and your right shoulder is immediately above it. (To turn right you put the right side of your body forwards into the turn, and to turn left you put the left side of your body forwards into the turn – the same as in any kind of turn.)
- Your right (inside) rein is in the open position held slightly into the circle (not back), elbow bent and maybe with your thumb pointing into the centre and your fingernails to the sky – an old and effective classical aid that invites a horse to flex and turn. You should just be able to see the outside corner of his eye and right nostril for correct flexion.
- Your left rein is pressed sideways (not back) on the horse's neck just in front of the withers. This turns the forehand. (In classical riding you 'push' the horse around a turn with the outside rein, never 'pull' with the inside rein.)
- Your outside leg is behind the girth and still, asking the hindquarters to stay in on the track.
- Your inside leg is supporting the horse on the girth asking for bend and, if necessary, maintaining the speed and impulsion.
- Finally, your mind is following the circular railway track, and your eyes are looking ahead a quarter of the way around the circle, and do so until it is finished. Always look ahead to where you want to go, remember: this is a very powerful aid.

All this sounds complicated, but in practice, it is simple and logical. With your body and aids in this position, your horse *will* perform a round 20m circle. The most important parts are the inside seat bone forwards, and looking around your circle; the other aids in support, though, will virtually guarantee perfection.

46 Improve the walk

In a good walk, whatever type it is, the horse should march forwards with purpose. Many horses mince along not even tracking up, let alone over-tracking. Quite a lot meander around, tripping over pebbles and admiring the scenery. Very few walk too fast. The old saying is that a horse should walk fast, trot slow and canter in between, and the next three topics consider this.

The importance of a good walk

A good, reaching-out, marching walk is always impressive to onlookers (and judges), and is a dream to sit on. If this comes naturally to your horse, then you should be thankful, because most of a horse's time under saddle should be spent in walk, the gait they use most in nature. A good walk eats up the ground effortlessly, does not jar the horse's legs, is easy for the rider to sit to, and is very unlikely to cause a horse problems, as can other gaits.

Another old saying is that walking is always beneficial, galloping rarely is.

A poor, unconvincing walk is usually the result of a combination of factors, including the horse not going forwards enthusiastically when asked, not reaching out from hip and shoulder, not maintaining the pace, and not walking straight, but wandering.

What can I do?

Insist that the horse goes forwards smartly, on the ground and under saddle, when asked, not three or four seconds later. Retrain 'forwards' in hand, if necessary. When mounted, give the horse a light aid by pushing forwards with the seat bones, and if you're expecting a delay, say 'walk on'. Wait two seconds and if he doesn't move off, give a firmer aid with the legs – brush firmly forwards with both legs, pinch or squeeze quickly (inwards, not backwards) and give the command 'walk on' again. If another two seconds elapses, repeat and tap with the whip. Most horses will be in walk by this time. Of course, the instant he moves forwards, say 'good boy'.

Have a comfortable contact on the reins, keep your seat and legs loose, and sense the purpose in his walk. Help him by looking and thinking towards where you want to go.

Achieve a good march by giving the leg aid till you get it, then praise him and sit with still legs. The instant he slows down, repeat the aid again, and so on till he maintains the speed with rhythm and purpose.

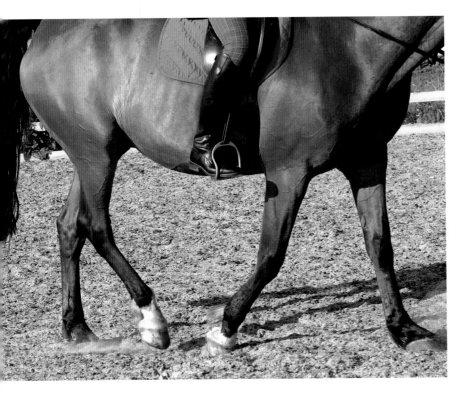

47 Improve the trot

The trot is the gait that is generally used for schooling. This is because it is an 'even' gait, the headcarriage is naturally fairly stable, and the pace itself favours impulsion and energy. Unfortunately, not many horses appear to know that, and whilst some trundle along aimlessly, others look as if they are in training for harness racing. There is a middle ground, however.

What is a good trot?

In a good working trot the horse will trot with purpose, energy and impulsion, but *not* speed. He will be comfortably accepting his bit, be light in hand, and flexed a little at the poll, pushing forwards from engaged hindquarters and tracking up (see right).

If your horse's trot is too slow with not much use of the hips and shoulders – maybe the horse is propping along or just too laid back – apply the aids as given for walk in the previous topic. Keep a gentle contact, but make sure that you are not transmitting tension or slow-down aids through the reins.

Have in your mind what you feel is your horse's natural rhythm, and aim to keep it with your rise but also to enhance the action. Exaggerate your rise with a definite rhythm, give him freedom of the head and use tapping, inward leg aids as you sit, maybe supported by occasional taps of the whip. Keep an upbeat attitude and encourage the horse vocally, and keep at it until you get your result. Then stop the aids, praise the horse, and subtly control the result with your outside rein. If he back pedals, repeat the aids, praise and so on.

The important things are not to let him ignore your leg, to keep a strong rhythm, and to vocally encourage him, stopping the aid and praising him when he complies.

If your horse's trot is too fast but probably without impulsion, imagine clearly him coming back to you and slowing down. 'Hold' the pace with your upper body and thighs, slow your rise with your seat, give repeated tweaks on your outside rein, half halts, and, if necessary, bring him back to walk for only two or three steps in order to break the impetus.

Set him off again and retain a very lazy, 'we're not going anywhere' attitude in your mind – do not mentally go with him in trot but expect him to come back to you. Circling usually slows horses down. Keep the rhythm, with the outside rein taking and giving, and praise him when he complies.

48 Improve the canter

The canter can be a heavenly gait to sit on when the horse is balanced, in control of his own body and light to the aids. But a lot of horses and riders have difficulties, if not actual problems, with canter, usually ones stemming from lack of balance. These include crookedness, marked one-sidedness, engagement just not happening, going on the forehand, and so on.

We can't seem to 'step up' a level

This complaint, plus all the niggling difficulties mentioned above, can usually be put down to one thing – lack of self-balance in the horse because the rider is not sitting to best advantage. *This is usually not the rider's fault* because riders are rarely taught how to sit specifically for canter.

What can I do?

When a horse is cantering, he begins a stride with his outside hind leg, let's say the left hind, for right canter. The next two legs come down as a pair – the right hind and left fore – and the final leg to land (misleadingly called 'the leading leg' because it looks as though the horse is pointing or leading the way with it) is the right fore. Then there is the moment of suspension.

This sequence of footfalls means that the two right legs land further forward than the two left ones. It also means that the right side of the horse's back is necessarily carried slightly in front of the left side during canter right, and vice versa.

The crucial inference of this is that, in order to sit in harmony with her horse and not, literally, at cross purposes with him, the rider's right seat bone and shoulder must be carried slightly in front of the left throughout canter right, and vice versa. In this way, the rider's body is not twisted and is in accord with that of her horse, making the whole

performance of canter easier, more logical and more comfortable for horse and rider, and recognized by the horse as 'keep cantering', particularly if the outside leg is back a little. The end result is far fewer difficulties and a relieved horse and rider!

To get back to trot, all you need do is return your inside seat bone to its normal position and the horse will trot. No other aid is needed.

The position which is usually taught – that the hips should be level with the horse's hips and the shoulders level with the horse's shoulders – would be fine if the instructor knew that the horse carried his back as

described above. Most, however, are themselves taught from diagrams showing a horse on a circle from above, with the inside hip and shoulder closer together than the outside ones. Their students, therefore, ride with the outside hip (and necessarily the seat bone) back and the inside hip forward, which is fine, but with the outside shoulder forward and the inside shoulder back. Their upper bodies are therefore twisted, and not in harmony with the way the horse goes in canter. This contorts their position in the saddle, which can be uncomfortable for them and the horse, and creates a great many problems.

49 Deal with common canter problems

Having mastered the position described on the preceding page, you will experience far fewer problems, but here are a few examples of queries based on questions I am frequently asked when teaching. Most problems are: the horse breaking into trot; the horse going too fast; the rider rocking backwards and forwards; and the horse banking in or motorbiking in canter.

Breaking into trot

This is mainly caused by the rider not sitting in balance, not staying in correct canter position, having a heavy feel on the inside rein so the horse does not feel able to flow on, or bumping around on the horse's back.

The rider should sit upright and centrally on her seat bones, with the seat and legs loose but 'toned' so there is no tension to disturb the horse's confidence or give him inadvertent aids. Sit with the inside seat bone forward and the outside leg back *from the hip*, more supportive than swinging it back from the knee.

Going too fast

This often puts a horse out of balance, on to the forehand and causes banking and falling in on the circle (see above).

Sit upright and drop the seat and legs round the horse. Picture to him a

very slow canter, 'hold' the pace with your upper body and thighs, and give rhythmic tweaks on the outside rein. Say a long drawn-out 'easy' and circle him smaller and smaller till he has to slow down. Then really praise him.

Rider rocks back and forth

The horse rocks up and down in the canter gait. As the inside hind lands to start the stride, the forehand rocks upwards, and rocks downwards as the leading foreleg lands. To counteract this, riders often let their upper bodies swing forward as the first hind leg lands and the forehand comes up, then backwards as the leading leg lands and the forehand rocks down.

The rider should sit bolt upright in all phases of canter (obviously not when going fast or jumping) and let the horse do the rocking underneath her

seat bones which act as a hinge. The hip joints play a vital role by allowing the thighs to move up and down with the horse's body whilst the rider's upper body remains upright and 'held'.

Horse banking in/ motorbiking

Horses' natural way to balance on smallish turns is to lean in (see bottom left). They are even more inclined to do this with a rider who 'goes with the horse' – in other words, leans in and makes matters worse.

The rider must sit erect, put her weight on the *outside* seat bone and stirrup and assume a correct canter position for the rein the horse is on. Also, slightly raise and carry inward (not backward) the inside hand, and squeeze it to ask for inward flexion. Keep the outside leg back from the hip and the inside one supporting down the girth.

79

50 Work on your halt – six ways to do it

It is surprising that halt causes so many problems. You'd think horses would be glad to stop! Instead, they grind to a halt, yaw on the bit, creep forwards, swing their quarters, fidget, leave their hind legs in the next county and do all sorts rather than flow forwards into a soft, still halt. What can be done to help? You've plenty of choice. Try these methods to find one that suits your horse.

Preliminaries

Although at the most basic level a pull on the reins means 'stop', you usually get an awful halt this way (see below). You have to learn not to pull blatantly on the reins. The halt is a downward transition and you should never ask for a transition of any sort if a horse is going badly in the present gait.

Therefore, have your horse going softly with his head lowered and flexed to the bit (top right). If your horse is pulling and yawing, say 'no' then 'head down', and give intermittent squeezes with the fingers on the inside rein, just as firm as you need to get a result, alternated with pinches

from the legs. Stop the aids and praise him when he obliges.

The three common factors when schooling halt, whatever method you are using are:

1 Always sit up straight and classically to halt, with no leaning or tilting forwards, backwards or to the side.
2 Say 'stand', which your horse should obey habitually.
3 Picture to your horse that you plan to halt, and look ahead, not down at him.

Do not, as is commonly taught, drive your horse forwards into halt with the legs if you want a light, willing halt, as

forward aids and stop aids at the same time are really confusing for the horse. I also do not like sitting down heavily in the saddle, again as is commonly done, as this can encourage some horses to flatten the back and discourage them from halting in correct posture with the back up and in a good vertebral bow.

Method 1 Sit still and centrally in the saddle (stop moving your body with the horse). Keep the hands still, as if you are trying to let the ground keep moving forwards under them and, if you do it gently and sensitively, the horse will stop smoothly up to his bit. The feel is not that of a pull, just a passive resistance.

Method 2 Tighten your seat and thigh muscles momentarily (which will lift you slightly up in the saddle) and turn both your thumbs outwards so that your fingernails are to the sky – an old, effective classical aid. A variation on this instead of tightening seat and thighs is to slightly stiffen or brace your upper body.

Method 3 Sit still. Push your elbows closely in to your sides, close your fingers on the reins, and block his movement with your shoulders. No pulling, of course.

Method 4 For this method you need to be able to feel under your seat which hind leg is moving forwards. As a hind leg comes forwards, the back on that side will dip downwards because it has lost its support. Keep your seat

and leg muscles completely loose and practise feeling for this.

Once you've got it, tighten your seat muscles alternately twice in co-ordination with the leg movement. So – as the left hind comes forwards tighten your left seat muscles, as the right hind comes forwards tighten your right seat muscles, then on the third beat tighten both sides and the horse will (almost certainly) stop square and up to his bridle. So it's left, right, both, and the horse stops in three steps. Your hands simply gently stay still and resist.

Method 5   Slightly raise your chest and move your upper body back infinitesimally, resist momentarily with your thighs and your hands, then relax and repeat if necessary (see right).

Method 6   My favourite. Just think and feel 'stand'. Try it!

51 Understand the half halt

There is an awful lot of confusion and lack of understanding about the half halt. In lessons, people do all sorts of things that they think are correct plus all sorts of things that they seem to have picked out of a bran tub, hoping they might have some effect. When asking clients what they do for half halt I am intrigued at the variety of techniques, which are usually nothing like their usual stop aids.

What exactly is a half halt?

It's simply half a halt – a suggestion of whatever halt aid you normally give, a sort of half-strength aid. As you should not need strong aids to stop anyway, the half halt is just a smidgeon of a request that most horses will respond to because they are familiar with your halt aid.

Just as different horses might respond better to one halt aid than another, so different half halts may be used. Usually, to avoid confusion and get a reliable response, it is best to use the same reduced aid for half halt as for a halt proper.

What is half halt used for?

1 For steadying an excited horse.
2 For slowing down any gait that is too fast.
3 For balancing a horse.
4 For getting the attention of an inattentive horse.
5 For gathering a horse a little more in hand.
6 Some people use it to check or warn a horse before asking for a specific movement.
7 As a preliminary reprimand on a horse who is taking liberties.
8 To get a standing horse to stand to attention rather than in an 'off duty' mode.

How do you do it exactly?

Just apply your halt aid (see previous topic) but lighter, and release it the instant you get whatever response you want, or when your horse is going a touch slower than you want. If the horse actually halts, you've given the aid too strongly or not released it quickly enough.

In training, it's as well to use a vocal command which always accompanies half halt so that the horse will differentiate between it and halt. I use 'stand' to accompany the halt and 'listen' for half halt. As with any vocal command, your horse should eventually respond just to that or just to the physical aid, whichever is appropriate to your circumstances.

52 Check results with give-and-take

A lot of people dread having to give and take the rein during a dressage test because they fear that the horse will fall apart or charge off. It is an excellent check on the correctness of the schooling because, at all levels of training, the horse must be able to go in self-balance and an appropriate, self-held posture for that level, otherwise something is going wrong.

Isn't self-carriage an advanced state?

No, it isn't. At every level of training we should aim to help the horse to be able to stand on his own four feet, and hold his head, neck and body in an appropriate posture for his level of education.

I find that conventionally trained, modern dressage horses are often heavy in hand, very reliant on being held together by the rider's legs and reins, and have been used to bits hoisted up holes too high. Being fortunate to be from a correct, classical background, I was amazed when, a few years ago, one national-level competitor told me that with bits adjusted like this, when she gives and takes the horse does not collapse because he thinks that she still has hold of the reins. I felt so sad for her horses.

How can I make give-and-take work correctly?

Adjust your bit logically and humanely (see topic 14). Have your horse going forwards (not fast, but with enjoyment, willingness and, as he progresses, oomph and impulsion). At his level, he needs to be answering your leg and hand aids well. When you sense that he is holding himself reasonably and is in balance – and not leaning on the bit at all – support and 'hold' him with your body, seat and legs and, keeping your elbows in place at your hips, completely open the bottom three fingers of both hands for a couple of seconds, then close them again.

What did he do, if anything? If the horse was going as described above, this will make no difference to his way of going – his posture, speed or balance. In that case, he is in self-balance or self-carriage for that level of training.

When he is *not* going as described above, by all means try give-and-take and you will find that he goes faster and/ or falls on the forehand and may even start forging. This confirms to you that he is not yet established in his work at that level. When performing give-and-take in competition you will need to put your hands actually forward (see right) or the judges may think that you have not done it.

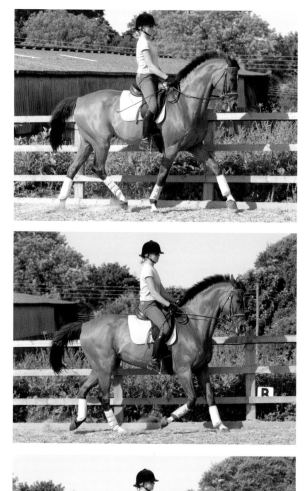
53 Learn to shorten the stride/collect

The way many riders attempt shortening of stride, and even collection which is more advanced, is to pull backwards with the reins whilst pushing forwards with the legs, with a view to slowing the horse down and driving him up to the hands and into a more pronounced outline. This may shorten the stride but at the expense of self-balance, correct posture and lightness.

What are the basic points to understand about shortening the stride?

This exercise is a fore-runner to actual collection. It is used to make a horse longitudinally manoeuvrable and responsive, to improve his balance and achieve lightness. It also helps develop and strengthen the muscles, in particular, of the back, loins, hindquarters and hind legs, and tightens those of the abdomen.

It should not be attempted by pulling the horse back by the bit and, horror of horrors, shortening his neck and maybe even having him go behind the bit or overbent, with the face behind the vertical.

Instead, slow him slightly with a half halt. *Then* ask with your legs for the hindquarters to engage and for the horse to lift within his carriage: this can be done effectively by squeezing upwards with your legs a couple of times – particularly in the suspension phase of trot – so that he goes with shorter, springier strides up to your controlling hand (particularly to the outside rein) but without tension and over-restriction.

Some say that the rhythm of the gait should not change, others that it is unreasonable to ask the horse to do this without slowing his rhythm a little. I feel that a slight slowing of rhythm helps the horse, especially in the early stages of learning this work.

Collection

Collection is achieved as the next stage, by the same means tactfully emphasized. The horse goes with the neck raised and arched but *not* shortened backwards (indeed pushed up and forwards) with the front of the face just in front of the vertical. The lower jaw is relaxed, the back up and the hindquarters well flexed downwards and engaged. The horse is physically in full control of himself, in as perfect balance as is possible, and ready and able to obey the rider's slightest aids in harmony.

54 Learn to lengthen the stride/extend

Flatwork

Many people ask for extension too early in training, before the horse is able to lengthen in a stable way and is soundly balanced in medium gaits. This prompts the rider to use too much bit contact in an effort to balance the horse. The horse usually goes with lack of engagement, a flattened back, hind legs not pushing under sufficiently and the forelegs flicking out (bottom photo) instead of arching forwards from the shoulder (top photo).

What are the basic points to understand?

Again, this is introductory to extension which is a quite advanced movement. Shortening of stride is taught before lengthening, and collection is taught before extension. Its advantages are to develop suppleness, also to teach the horse to stretch out and really use his body whilst remaining balanced and in control, and able to come back to an ordinary (medium) walk or working trot or canter without going crookedly or losing balance.

The horse needs to be well established in going forwards from the leg on request and able to do so whilst remaining light in hand, in good posture and self-balance before being asked to lengthen (top photo).

To get the horse to lengthen his stride, establish him in a good, ordinary (medium) walk, so he is light in hand, in self-balance but going up to his bit and comfortably in hand.

First allow a longer neck and head posture by opening your fingers a little, then ask with your legs just behind the girth for more energy from the hind legs. Encourage the horse by moving your seat bones alternately forwards with each hind leg on the same side – as the left hind comes forwards (you should feel the back on that side dip) allow your left seat bone to go forwards and up a little. Do not keep asking with the leg once the horse has lengthened unless he shortens again. To bring him back, apply a half halt.

Extension

Not only must the horse be able to lengthen well before he is asked to extend, he must also be well established in medium gaits. Do not be in too much of a rush to perform actual extended gaits because you can risk the horse's trust in you, teach him to rush out of control, and he may lose his balance and start to lean on your hand. Most people really need a knowledgeable trainer at this level.

55 Understand transitions

Transitions not only test your schooling but are a useful schooling device in themselves. Poor transitions are proof of the work not being properly established, lack of suppleness and self-control in the horse, and lack of tact and clarity from the rider. As schooling exercises, they enhance concentration and attention, improve balance, develop muscles and increase control.

From gait to gait

As a trainer, it is important to understand the reasons for the importance of transitions. Transitions are changes in a horse's way of going from gait to gait or movement to movement but, as shown on the next page, they also apply within gaits.

With a horse you are tuned in to (and a sensitive trainer does not need much time for this), you can easily achieve transitions of all kinds by picturing mentally to your horse what you want him to do and by using your body and seat in particular ways (covered in individual topics throughout this book). The important thing is to

realize that transitions are achieved with the mind, body and seat supported by the use or mere positioning of the legs and hands/reins.

What can I do?

- Read in this book about the transitions you want under the topics covering the gaits concerned.
- Get used to imagining or 'picturing to your horse' what you are asking for – a horse who obeys his rider's mental messages exhibits the ultimate in lightness.
- Check your aids so you are sure that you are asking correctly and not confusing or inhibiting your horse. If your horse does not get the message, or you then prevent him complying, it is not his fault.
- Remember that transitions are performed by the horse's 'engine', his hindquarters. Transitions performed with the horse on the forehand, out of balance or without sufficient 'drive' from behind, will not succeed or will be poor.

Within gaits

Transitions within gaits involve slowing down or speeding up, or changing from a free gait on a loose rein, working on a long rein (not the same) plus, depending on your discipline and abilities, collected, working, medium and extended ways of going.

What can I do? One of the most important abilities to cultivate is to be able to picture to your horse what you want and, in downward transitions, to learn to 'hold' your horse with your body, thighs and hands as you slightly resist his forward movement. Think 'slow' and slow the rhythm of your seat as you follow his gait.

With a horse who has been driven too fast in trot (a very common error confused with impulsion), you can even think firmly 'stand' or 'rein back' as you hold with your body, then, just as he reaches a speed in the existing gait which is a little slower than you want, let him go on fractionally, repeating if he speeds up again.

For upward transitions within gaits, a simple push forwards with the seat bones is enough for a well schooled horse (being sure to control your upper body so that you do not lean backwards in a 'driving' seat). If this is not enough, brush forwards with the inside leg, or both if necessary, or give a slight forward nudge with the insides of the calves. Release slightly with the fingers to allow for the increase, without the horse losing his posture.

The voice in transitions

For downward transitions within gaits say "easy" and for upward transitions perhaps say the horse's name and maybe click or say "go on" in an encouraging tone.

56 Get accurate canter strike-offs

Flatwork

This transition really can cause a lot of problems to a lot of horses and riders. People and their horses get into a real tizzy about it, horses develop a 'thing' about it, riders avoid doing it because they know they're going to have a problem and it becomes a no-go area in a lot of cases – other than out hacking when the horse will go willingly into canter without a problem!

before the corner. Look ahead and around your corner. Keep your inside rein very light (see left) because it often helps to let the horse look to the outside of his bend, as at liberty. Once the strike-off is established, you can start to ask for straightness, then inside flexion.

Keep your upper body very still and erect with your inside shoulder forward above your seat bone, and relax your mind, seat and legs. Keeping your inside seat bone and shoulder forward, slide your outside leg back a little from the hip and squeeze with it, saying 'canter'. Do not force the horse to look to the inside and you are highly likely to get a canter strike-off.

Try in different corners, on bends and circles, and on the other rein of course. Ultimately you should go for straight-line strike-offs.

If it makes you feel better...

I regularly ride a Fell pony and teach her very experienced rider. We both have trouble sometimes with canter strike-off on either leg because it depends entirely on what mood the pony is in as to whether or not she will give us the correct leg, despite knowing very well what we're asking for. This pony has been ridden by an international classical trainer and he had the same problem. (She has been thoroughly checked physically so we accept that it's all in her head – keeping us in our places.)

Why does it happen?

Failure to strike off into canter correctly, or at all, is often because the rider is sitting badly, the rider is worried about it, the horse is in the wrong balance, there is too much pressure on the inside rein, or the horse was not confirmed in striking off into canter from a voice command on the lunge, the lunge rider gradually taking over from the trainer.

What can I do?

First, re-read the topics covering canter, especially how to sit in canter and why (topics 48 and 49).

Have your horse in a working trot sitting, in good posture, and plan to ask for canter before a corner, which makes things easier as the corner supports him. Warn him that you are going to canter by pushing your inside seat bone forwards and imagining to him that you are both going to canter

---

Flatwork

56 Get accurate canter strike-offs

This transition really can cause a lot of problems to a lot of horses and riders. People and their horses get into a real tizzy about it, horses develop a 'thing' about it, riders avoid doing it because they know they're going to have a problem and it becomes a no-go area in a lot of cases – other than out hacking when the horse will go willingly into canter without a problem!

before the corner. Look ahead and around your corner. Keep your inside rein very light (see left) because it often helps to let the horse look to the outside of his bend, as at liberty. Once the strike-off is established, you can start to ask for straightness, then inside flexion.

Keep your upper body very still and erect with your inside shoulder forward above your seat bone, and relax your mind, seat and legs. Keeping your inside seat bone and shoulder forward, slide your outside leg back a little from the hip and squeeze with it, saying 'canter'. Do not force the horse to look to the inside and you are highly likely to get a canter strike-off.

Try in different corners, on bends and circles, and on the other rein of course. Ultimately you should go for straight-line strike-offs.

If it makes you feel better...

I regularly ride a Fell pony and teach her very experienced rider. We both have trouble sometimes with canter strike-off on either leg because it depends entirely on what mood the pony is in as to whether or not she will give us the correct leg, despite knowing very well what we're asking for. This pony has been ridden by an international classical trainer and he had the same problem. (She has been thoroughly checked physically so we accept that it's all in her head – keeping us in our places.)

Why does it happen?

Failure to strike off into canter correctly, or at all, is often because the rider is sitting badly, the rider is worried about it, the horse is in the wrong balance, there is too much pressure on the inside rein, or the horse was not confirmed in striking off into canter from a voice command on the lunge, the lunge rider gradually taking over from the trainer.

What can I do?

First, re-read the topics covering canter, especially how to sit in canter and why (topics 48 and 49).

Have your horse in a working trot sitting, in good posture, and plan to ask for canter before a corner, which makes things easier as the corner supports him. Warn him that you are going to canter by pushing your inside seat bone forwards and imagining to him that you are both going to canter

88

57 Achieve rein-back with the lightest of aids

Flatwork

This is another movement that causes a good deal of *angst* among horses and riders. The problem is that most riders think that the combined (conflicting) aids of pulling back on the mouth plus forward leg aids 'to push the horse forward up to his bit' will send the horse backwards – but it doesn't. It confuses him, and I am sure hurts his mouth, too.

Understanding the rein-back

I class rein-back as one of those essential manoeuvrability movements and teach it as soon as the horse is established in going forward reliably to a leg aid. Any horse which does not go smartly forward on request or, worse, uses going backwards as an evasion, as an objection to immobility or to discipline (all of which can develop into napping) should certainly not yet be taught rein-back.

Rein-back that is done correctly increases the strength of the muscles of the back and hindquarters and tests the horse's co-operation with his rider because it is not an easy exercise for him to perform under weight, and it is a submissive action in nature.

The rein-back is a two-time gait, the legs moving backwards in diagonal pairs. Therefore, it is not a backwards walk but more like a backwards trot without the speed or the moment of suspension. The legs should make a firm one-two-one-two beat and the

horse should not be allowed to creep or to shuffle backwards. This indicates a lack of correct posture and balance, and a failure to accept the bit.

How should I do it?

First, reliably establish the rein-back in hand (see topic 24) and make sure the horse will back to the vocal command.

Your aim is to transfer this level of co-operation to the saddle. The specific aids described below, plus the horse's obedience to the word 'back' and, if possible, a sensible friend on hand, will achieve success surprisingly quickly.

Come to a halt with your horse softly flexed to the bit and standing square. Lighten your seat by rising slightly in the saddle and leaning forwards just a little; this helps to take weight away from the hindquarters. Give a *backwards* brushing aid with the insides of your calves, say 'back', and then give a *gentle* but unmistakable intermittent squeeze on the reins. *Do not pull backwards on them.* Your friend can help at this point by placing the flat of her hand on your horse's chest and giving little pushes.

At the very first inkling of a backward step, say 'good boy', and walk forwards at once in order to establish forward movement. Repeat this a few times till he shows a clear understanding of the aids and steps back confidently. One step backwards at this stage is a good leap forwards!

58 Use counter canter for suppling, strengthening and obedience

There's a lot more to counter canter than cantering round 'on the wrong leg'. Many people cannot see the uses of it and even avoid it. Some do not know at what stage to introduce it or how to get into it, or out of it, come to that. Like most aspects of schooling, there is no mystique to it, and counter canter is a great suppling exercise when done well.

When is the horse ready to learn counter canter?

The horse must first be capable of performing easily all the movements listed in the schooling progression at the beginning of this section. He should have a well established rhythm (not erratic) and steady tempo (not speeding up and slowing down unless asked). He should accept the bit and go comfortably in hand with correct poll flexions and body 'bend' on circles and turns.

His circles should be true and he should not slow down on turns. He must be straight, not evasive, absolutely obedient to the aids and going forwards. He should be capable of correct 10m to 12m circles in walk and trot and 15m circles in canter.

He *must* be reliably obedient to the canter aids and strike off on the correct leg without fail, otherwise counter canter will cause him confusion. He must not change legs, break back to trot or go disunited.

Counter canter is taught before flying change because otherwise the horse will change legs unbidden and it will be difficult for both of you.

How do I introduce counter canter?

Method 1   To introduce only one or two strides of counter canter, bring your horse round the school in working canter on the outside track and turn down the next long side on to the inside track. The canter must be correct, easy and balanced and you must be sitting in the correct position for the rein you are on.

Your inside seat bone will stay forward, but now slightly weight your outside stirrup and seat bone; remember that where you put your weight the horse will go. Also move him over to the track by pressing with your inside leg at the girth. Your outside leg slightly back and just touching the horse confirms that inside flexion is still required. Your inside rein maintains the inside flexion and your outside one is held in a slightly open position away from the neck to lead him over to the track, returning to the neck as soon as he reaches it.

Say 'good boy' the instant that he moves over, whilst maintaining the correct bend and leg. Repeat on the other rein, then let your horse have a break and a full stretch down to the ground. You can gradually ask for more counter canter by eventually bringing the horse down the long side at the quarter or three-quarter line.

Method 2   In, say, left canter, at K ride half of a 15m circle, the deepest part of which reaches the track just before A. On completion of the half circle, canter diagonally across the school heading for the track between E and H. As your horse turns slightly to reach and proceed along the track, maintain left canter (aids as above) and he will perform a step or two of counter canter before straightening out on the track, still in left canter. Once on the track, return your left seat bone level with your right to bring the horse back to trot, and trot round the corner.

Method 3   Use a shallow loop along a long side. At first, make the loop only to the inside track and back to the track, then extend it to the quarter line as the horse's competence increases.

Canter right and leave the track just after, say, M and perform the first part of your loop, the deepest part being level with B. Then, maintain right canter (aids as above) and, in counter canter, rejoin the track just before F, cantering round the FA corner in normal right canter.

You will doubtless devise your own gentle introductions to this useful movement. Just don't overdo your demands as you enhance your horse's capabilities, as this is not an easy exercise for him and he will rely heavily on your correct position and aids for direction and reassurance. An excellent counter canter is shown here. Timmy is in right canter, flexed right and clearly travelling left, where Abi is looking.

59 Build towards flying changes

At a Richard Maxwell evening a few years ago, he asked how many of the packed audience had done flying changes. I was stunned to see fewer than half-a-dozen hands go up. He picked a member of the audience who had never done one, and within a couple of minutes on his horse she was doing them repeatedly and easily – to the extent that he couldn't get her to dismount!

Aren't flying changes terribly advanced?

Horses don't think so. They do them every day in the field when playing about, and quite often under saddle when we don't ask them. They are the natural way for a cantering or galloping horse to change direction, or give his muscles on one lead a rest by changing to the other. Racehorses do them quite often for this latter reason.

How do I go about it?

A horse should be able to canter easily under saddle, balanced and with his hindquarters engaged, before you introduce flying changes, otherwise you may get rough changes, the horse may change in front but not behind and go disunited. He needs to be responsive to your aids, of course.

Method 1   Canter in a balanced, engaged canter in a 20m circle at one end of the school. Coming towards X, come down to trot and canter on the other leg just after X. Gradually reduce the number of trot strides until you feel the time is right and the horse is almost waiting for it. Then, at a moment of suspension in canter as you turn at about X, maintaining your balance and sitting upright, subtly reverse your position and your canter aids in mid-air, remembering to look in the new direction, and your horse is very likely to change.

Method 2   Similarly to Method 1, as you turn at about X, say from right canter to left canter, in the moment of suspension simply block your horse on the right by applying your right leg and rein sideways against his side and neck respectively and think left and, again, you'll probably get it.

Method 3   On a horse with a very well balanced, engaged and accomplished canter, you can do a flying change simply by reversing your seat bones. Canter in a right circle in normal canter right position, concentrating on having your right seat bone forward. As you canter over X, in the moment of suspension simply put your left seat bone forward and look left, and a horse who goes from the seat as a matter of course (which I believe should always be our aim) will change.

How wonderful to be able to do a flying change without all the kinking and kicking so often seen at dressage competitions!

60 Ride to music

The right kind of music really enhances a horse's performance and enjoyment under saddle, even if his strides are not exactly matched to the music. Dési Lorent, my teacher of the 1980s, used to have classical music playing most of the time during lessons, and horses, riders and onlookers all found it uplifting and relaxing.

What's the best way to go about it?

Some people ride to music via earphones from a unit in their pocket but this deprives the horse and any onlookers of its benefit. A portable CD player is probably the most practical way of arranging musical accompaniment as you ride, though if you are fortunate enough to have access to an indoor school you may be able to go for something more permanent, such as piping it through the sound system.

What's the best kind of music?

Experiments in Ireland many years ago showed that horses did not like any kind of thudding, raucous music such as disco music or what I call 'tinned music' often played in supermarkets and similar places. They did respond to soft and soothing music, or more upbeat and cheerful but not loud or grating music (if it can be called that).

I remember reading also somewhere that horses are not keen on the sound of violins but like full orchestras, they don't like jazz or heavy metal and the like, trumpets and bugles excite them (even if they haven't been in the army) and they prefer instrumental music to vocals. So, there's plenty to choose from.

Get the beat

Although working out your own routine and editing tapes and so on is very time-consuming and complex, you can choose a selection of tunes which roughly correspond to your horse's normal walk, trot and canter rhythms and will probably find that your horse will at least try to follow the rhythm. Then working out a simple routine of movements to them will be great fun. There are music studios in most areas now that should be able to help you devise something not too complicated or expensive. Working to music certainly perks horses up and calms them down at the same time, and anything which makes them feel good is well worth a try.

Lateral work

Sideways on

Lateral work is another of those aspects of riding that has an undeserved stratospheric aura. So many people have never moved a single step sideways on their horses, on purpose anyway, and cannot see the reason for it. Others have tried it without really knowing how to approach it, or appreciating what it is for, have struggled with it, and then written it off.

Like other aspects of equitation, it falls into place if the rider understands what she is about, even at a basic level, and the horse has been properly prepared by means of a logical schooling progression (*see* p. 51). The progression given on this page is basic but dependable; others may differ slightly, but on the whole, they won't be far apart.

I should repeat here that you need to be a pretty good rider before you can think of schooling a horse. This book contains basic information designed to give such riders a good start in schooling work, using methods that are not confrontational or forceful, which are logical, and which work in practice. Horses take to them easily and willingly.

Lateral work needs approaching correctly, like anything else. It is an important part of a good riding horse's education because it engages both his body and his brain. It also has a beneficial effect on his mind, which is not the same as his brain. You will find that the more that horses are taught, the more they think about their work, and the more they are able to use what they have learned in both their work and their off-duty lives. The horse of a friend of mine taught himself to manipulate gates, once he had been taught turns on the forehand and haunches; and another, having learned to engage her hindquarters under saddle, now uses the technique to whirl round on her hind legs without warning, and set off up inviting tracks when she feels like going for a spin.

It is true that when teaching horses anything we can only build on what they can naturally do. You only have to watch youngsters at liberty to see the full range of movements we later try so earnestly to teach them, including lateral work. This proves that the difficulties are caused by us – our weight and our possibly confused, and confusing, aids.

Lateral work builds up muscles that are barely affected by other work, making a well muscled and more fully and evenly developed horse. It makes horses use their brains to think where to put their feet, increasing agility and strength, and it makes them lighter and more manoeuvrable under saddle, and so handier and even more fun to ride. The earlier lateral movements facilitate the development of collection.

Here is a suggested progression for *basic* lateral work. It can be brought in after no. 6 in the progression on p. 51: that is, once the horse can change rein in balance with correct, slight flexions at walk and trot. You need a good feel to decide when to integrate the movements in both progressions, and it may vary from one horse to another. An empathetic teacher would be a great help, and see Further Reading on p. 150.

1 Turn on or about the forehand

2 Turn on or about the haunches/hindquarters

3 Walk pirouette

4 Shoulder-fore and shoulder-in

5 Leg-yield

6 Shoulder-out (counter shoulder-in)

61 Understand 'SO.SI.LY'

What does *that* mean? SO.SI.LY stands for 'Shoulder-Out, Shoulder-In and Leg-Yield'. In these three basic lateral movements, the horse does *not* look where he is going, and it is *so silly* not to look where you are going. It is just a little phrase to help you remember them, because riders are often unsure about the direction in which the horse flexes in these movements.

Why not look where you are going?

It is not so much a matter of looking where you are going, but of what stresses you are placing on your horse's body. It is quite natural for horses to appear not to look where they are going when they turn or do a few sideways steps. As herbivorous prey animals, their eyes are set on each side of their head rather than in front like ours, and each eye has a wider but shallower view of the world than a human eye. This means that equines can see almost all round themselves, so looking in the direction in which they are going is not essential for them to actually *see* where they are going.

The horse's horizontally formed and balanced body has a tremendous balancing aid on its front end – the neck and head. His notional centre of mass, gravity or balance is inside his chest just behind the elbow about a third of the

way up from the breastbone. Although the horse's 'engine' is his hindquarters, his steering gear is his shoulders and, as you may have noticed, horses often do not look where they are going when at liberty: the head and neck usually sway in the opposite direction, even if only slightly, though more so at speed, to balance the trunk.

This natural biomechanical system makes it logical, and easier for the horse, to flex away from the direction of movement in these three early lateral movements. It also means that there is no stretch demanded on the side of the body which is pushing the horse away along his route. The inside legs are those on the side of the body to which the horse is flexed, and the inside hind, in particular, has to step well under and across in these three movements and then push the body away, and it is easier for the horse to manage this when not experiencing stretch as well.

It's just horse sense, really.

Shoulder-out
three track

Shoulder-in
three track

Leg yield

62 Use corners to introduce lateral movement

How can corners possibly help with lateral movement? Many horses and riders have enough trouble as it is making correct turns and corners with the horse going straight, hind hooves following fore, without making life difficult by asking for lateral movement as well. In practice, however, moving around a corner does make achieving a sideways step or two easy.

Please explain

When on a turn or circle (a turn being a segment of a circle), the horse is already thinking, and flexed/bent, to the inside, so asking him to keep his forehand flexed inwards to that side as you reach the straight part of the track is no big deal. If you maintain this slight lateral position, but ask him to carry on up the straight arena fence for a step or two, rather than continuing on the track of the turn or circle, you will surely get a lateral step or two.

How exactly do I do that?

- Coming into a corner in a forward-going, ordinary walk, say on the right rein, sit as you normally would for a right-hand bend or circle, with your right (inside) seat bone and shoulder forward. This is your main directional aid. You can support it with your outside leg back slightly from the hip. Your face and glance should be directed between the horse's ears.

- Invite your horse round the corner with a right/inside open rein – your inside hand lifting slightly and moving in (not back). With the left/outside rein, apply a little sideways pressure on the neck just in front of the withers to ask the forehand to move across to the right.

- As you come out of the corner on to the straight, *keep this position for a stride until the forehand is off the track* (see right). Then change your seat and shoulder position only: put your outside (left) seat bone and shoulder forward up the track, weight the seat bone slightly, and look up the track with your eyes, but keep your face directed between the ears.

- Your rein aids will keep the forehand off the track to the right but your left seat bone, right leg and eyes will now send the horse up the track for a step or two. Instantly say 'good boy' but do not stroke him as this will destroy his guidance from the reins. He's new to this, remember.

Then you can either:
a reverse your seat bones, pushing the inside one forward, and your horse will continue off on to a circle; or
b you can simply bring both seat bones level, press on the girth with your inside leg, and straighten your rein aids, and the horse will walk straight up the track.

Praise him instantly. Repeat it on the next corner, then a couple of times similarly on the other rein.

63 Start with turn on/ about the forehand

Turn on or about the forehand is the first lateral movement to teach a horse, partly because it is fairly easy for the horse to do, and partly because it gives the rider control of the horse's powerhouse or engine – his hindquarters. It loosens the hips and develops the hind-leg muscles. Moving the quarters to the side is most useful in preventing running back or rearing.

About turn on the forehand

In this movement the horse is asked for a turn on the forehand to the right or left. A turn to the right (see right) has the horse flexed right and the hindquarters moving left away from the inside (right) leg, so the horse is, in effect, turning right; and vice versa.

In the turn about the forehand, the horse describes a very small circle with the forefeet, whereas in a turn on the forehand the horse picks up and puts down his inside foreleg on the same spot whilst the outside one circles round it: this is more difficult to achieve.

A turn on/about the forehand may be a quarter turn of 90 degrees, a half turn of 180 degrees, or a full turn of 360 degrees (not often required).

How do we do it?

The horse must first be obedient on the ground to turning away from the rider's hand accompanied by the word 'over'. The horse must also be willingly accepting the bit in his work.

- Bring your horse to a square halt with him softly in hand and flexed at the poll.
- For a turn to the left, flex him slightly left so that you can just see the corner of his eye and nostril. Your inside leg is held back a little from the hip and placed behind the girth, and the outside one is placed at the girth.

Press rhythmically against the horse's side with your inside leg, saying 'over' (ideally with your heel down).
- Your horse must cross his inside hind in front of the outside one, though many move the outside leg away first and bring the inside one up to it. This is incorrect, as it does not supple and strengthen the hind legs and quarters in the same way.
- A sensible friend tapping the inside

hock with a schooling whip may be helpful in early attempts.
- Bringing the inside rein over in front of the withers towards the rider's outside hip (called indirect rein), with a gentle but distinct pulsing contact, also has the effect of turning the quarters to the outside (the right in this case, using left inside rein). Instantly say 'good boy' for success.

64 Next try turn on/ about the haunches and walk pirouette

This second exercise is a little more difficult than turn on the forehand, as the horse must shift his weight back to accomplish it, therefore it improves his balance. It supples the fore legs and forehand, strengthens the whole body, and gives the rider 'steering' control. It can help to prevent or deal with bucking, shying, spinning, and planting the forefeet.

About turn on the haunches

All preliminary lateral schooling exercises (turns on the forehand/haunches, shoulder-in/-out and leg-yield) performed properly on both reins help with the common problem of 'one-sidedness' in horses, because they get the horse used to flexion, weight adjustment, stretching and crossing the legs in a fairly undemanding way; but I think that turn on the haunches and shoulder-in help most.

The reason for one-sidedness, where a horse flexes and goes easily on one rein but awkwardly on the other, is because the muscles on the 'soft', easy side are slightly contracted or shortened all the time. This is because horses use and go mainly towards their favourite side when free to do so. When asked to stretch those muscles in flexing to the opposite side, they find it a little uncomfortable. Dismounted passive and active stretches will certainly help, but so will turn on the haunches and shoulder-in.

The horse flexes towards the direction of the turn and crosses his outside foreleg over the inside, in a 90-, 180- or 360-degree turn (a quarter, half or full pirouette). The inside hind foot lifts up and down on the same spot or a little in front of it, and the outside hind foot forms a small circle around it (see right).

How do I do it?

You can introduce it at halt, but ultimately it should be done from a good in-hand or collected walk, preceded by a gentle half halt.

- Come to a halt, initially along the fence or hedge as this will help control the quarters, with the horse softly in hand and flexed at the poll.
- Sitting up and very correctly, push your inside seat bone (weighted a little) and shoulder forward, and flex the horse gently to the inside with a light, open inside rein.

- With your face directed between the ears and looking to the inside, gently but clearly push or tap the horse's forehand over to the inside with the outside leg just behind the girth and the outside rein nudging sideways just in front of the withers. Your inside leg is for the horse to bend around, and to nudge him to ask for movement. Initially, a sensible friend tapping his outside knee with a schooling whip can help.

As always, the instant you get even the semblance of movement, say 'good boy'. At first, be happy with one step. Then repeat, and ask again on the other rein.

65 Work on shoulder-in/-fore

Shoulder-in is the master lateral schooling exercise that leads towards collection. Like no other, it supples (loosens), strengthens, balances and teaches collection. We start with shoulder-fore ridden with inside flexion at a less than 30-degree angle to the fence, progressing gradually to the advanced four-track shoulder-in at 45 degrees, ultimately working away from the fence, and on turns and circles.

About shoulder-fore and shoulder-in

The fact that these exercises are so important and valuable – indeed, they are the key to a correctly developed riding horse – is no reason to be nervous or apprehensive of them. The method given here is logical, and always works first time with no confusion.

The shoulder-in is ridden on three or (more advanced) four tracks, and the shoulder-fore approaches three tracks.

Four-track shoulder-in (see p. 101) The two front hooves make individual tracks in from the outside track of the school, and the two hind hooves also make individual tracks. So for right shoulder-in, you are on the right rein going down a long side of the manège, and your horse's hooves, from the outside track inwards, are: left hind, right hind, left fore, right fore.

Three-track shoulder-in The hoof positions from the outside track inwards are: left hind, right hind following left fore on the same track, and right fore.

Shoulder-fore The hoof positions from the outside track inwards will be: left hind, left fore close to it, right hind just in from it, and right fore. Be happy with a very little, but clear, lateral movement. A knowledgeable friend on the ground can help here.

Starting these exercises at walk is physically more difficult for the horse because his muscles have to work harder to push him sideways, not having the impetus and spring of trot to help him travel. However, it gives both rider and horse time to think about it all. Once you've got the hang of it, trot is actually easier and develops agility more than strength. Shoulder-in can be performed in canter by advanced horses.

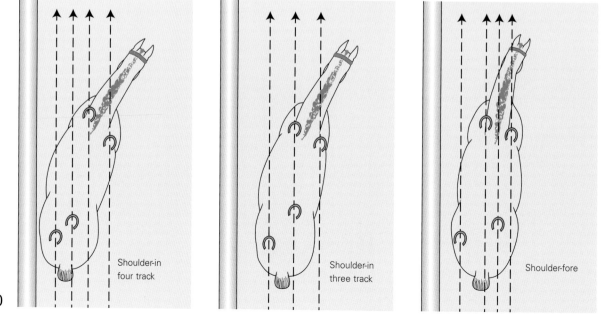

Shoulder-in four track

Shoulder-in three track

Shoulder-fore

How do I do it?

Don't worry about precise hoof placements when you are just starting. To perform a shoulder-fore on a long side for the first time, proceed as follows:

- You are on the right rein. Come along a short side in ordinary walk with the horse marching forwards comfortably in hand and flexed at the poll.
- In the corner, stay on one track and do a 10m circle, looking between the horse's ears. You will be in position right with your inside (right) seat bone and shoulder forwards into the turn, the horse bent softly right.
- As you complete the circle and come back on to the long side, keep your seat bone and shoulder forward, and pretend that you are going to do another circle, to bring your horse's forehand slightly off the outside track.
- As soon as it is off the track, keep your horse flexed to the inside (right) but switch your seat bones around and put your outside (left) seat bone and shoulder forwards pointing up the outside track, and turn your eyes (not your face) up the track, picturing to your horse that that is where you are both going.
- Your horse will change his route (at which point it is important that you say 'good boy') and, staying bent round your inside (right) leg (remember he flexes away from the direction of movement in shoulder-in), will travel slightly sideways up the track with the inside fore slightly crossing the outside one.

The above is the simplest and most basic technique, although there are extra things you can do to help:

- You need to keep your horse's flexion slightly to the inside (right).
- You should keep your outside leg just behind the girth, as on the circle, and your inside leg down the girth, pressing the horse up the track, your face directed between his ears and, most effectively…
- …you can slightly weight your outside (left) seat bone and stirrup. Remember that where you put your weight, and where you look, your horse will go.

In relation to weight, when doing shoulder-fore on a circle, your weight is on the *inside* seat bone and stirrup, otherwise your horse will drift out of the circle. Look well round your circle and keep the horse's forehand flexed in off the circle with your outside rein. Your outside leg should be positioned just behind the girth to keep the hind feet on the circle track, and to stop the quarters from swinging out.

101

66 Work on shoulder-out/counter shoulder-in

Shoulder-out, or counter shoulder-in, is less familiar than shoulder-in, but serves similar purposes and makes horses 'thoughtfully versatile', according to an acquaintance of mine. This is another exercise in which the horse is flexed away from the direction of movement. It is performed with the head flexed to the fence, rather than into the school as in shoulder-in.

About shoulder-out

Shoulder-out should be performed once the horse is competent at shoulder-in. It, too, can be ridden on four tracks or less. Horses (and riders) do find it more difficult because the fence is not guiding the hindquarters but the head, which does not feel so supportive. Because of this, many horses fall in away from the fence so the rider has to be extra vigilant with their leg and outside rein aids.

The main difficulty that people have with starting this exercise is that their mind-set is still on shoulder-in, and they come into it in the same way, from a circle on the same rein. *Then* they try to work out how to achieve an outside bend, thereby confusing both themselves and their horses in the process.

So how do I do it?

Think it through. You need to come at it the opposite way round.

- Walk on, say, the left rein down a long side, and at the end in the corner, perform a demi-volte (an 8m half circle), in left flexion with the left seat bone forward obviously, followed by a straight line, still in left flexion, towards the outside track you were just on.
- When your horse's head is nearly above the outside track (and don't make him bump his nose on the fence!), *maintaining left flexion*, switch your seat bones around again – and your shoulders above them – so that your right seat bone and shoulder come forward and point up the long side. Weight your right seat bone and look with your eyes up the track, keeping your face angled between the horse's ears. Your horse will move laterally in shoulder-out up the long side. The instant he makes a correct move say 'good boy'; he needs this reassurance.
- To dissuade your horse from drifting into the school, keep up the bend and impulsion with your inside leg. Maintain the head in left flexion with gentle squeezes on the left rein, and keep the right rein and leg close to the horse's neck and girth to aid bend.

- Come out of it by bringing your right seat bone and shoulder back level with your left, and allowing your left rein forward by opening your fingers, so releasing the flexion. The horse will naturally straighten up and take the outside track, especially if you keep looking up it.

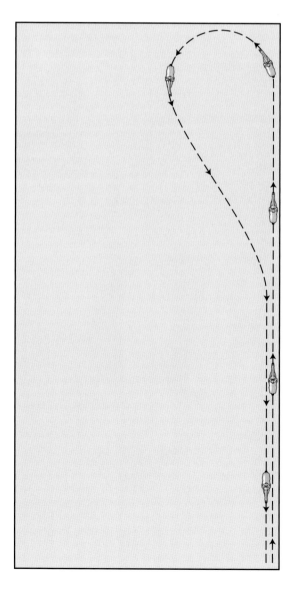

67 Work on leg-yield

Lateral work

Leg-yield is not one of my favourite exercises, and not only because it is not a traditional, classical movement. I find that, despite the aids and bend being different, a lot of horses become confused between leg-yield and half-pass as they are both done so often on the arena diagonal. I use leg-yield less and less, although I do teach it to clients who request it.

Why do leg-yield?

It does have a purpose in that it teaches the horse to move away from inside leg pressure whilst he is moving more freely than in turn on the forehand, which teaches the same thing. Both turn on the forehand and leg-yield should not be performed much once the horse obeys the inside leg, unless their lessons need re-establishing.

Turn on the forehand puts the horse's weight on the forehand, which is usually just what we don't want, although this is sometimes useful in foiling rearing and running backwards. Leg-yield can cause confusion between it and half-pass, although it can have a strengthening and suppling purpose; however, these can be achieved in less confusing ways.

What form does leg-yield take?

The horse flexes away from the direction of movement, and the movement itself is normally done out to the track of one long side, mostly in walk or trot, the horse moving forwards and sideways, and the inside legs (on the side of the flexion) crossing over the outside ones (see right). The horse should arrive at the track with shoulders and quarters level, neither leading, the major fault being that the flexion is overdone and the outside shoulder falls out to the track, even to the extent that the legs do not cross at all but the horse just goes in a straight line.

How do I do it correctly?

- Start in ordinary walk, and on the right rein, bring your horse on to the inside track flexed softly and slightly to the right. (You can eventually do it from the quarter or centre lines.)
- Turn your eyes towards the track. Your outside leg at the girth helps to prevent the shoulder leading, and your outside seat bone is weighted and slightly forward.
- Your outside rein plays a major role in controlling the outside shoulder, too, by pressing on the neck just in front of the withers.
- Your inside rein gently maintains a *slight* flexion, and your inside leg, just behind the girth, pulses in a squeezing or tapping movement, to ask the horse to travel to the track.

103

68 Think about travers

Travers and renvers take us beyond basic work, but it is as well to consider them and their place in more advanced schooling, even though this book is aimed at getting you going at a basic level. If you don't aim higher you'll never progress. As in so many aspects of riding, experts disagree about which exercise is the most difficult and exactly when each one should be taught.

About travers

Travers (pronounced *tra-vair*) is performed head to the wall or fence, with the horse flexed in the direction of movement, *looking where he is going*, because it is not one of the SO.SI.LY movements. You can remember which is travers by thinking T for travers, T for teeth – teeth to the wall = travers.

Travers and renvers are usually taught after shoulder-in and -out and leg-yield (if used).

Travers is a great suppling exercise, and is the standard preparation for half-pass. Although ultimately the horse should form a 45-degree angle with the fence (some say less) – see left – you can start with much less than this, no more than a nuance of carrying the quarters in (on request) from the outside track. Before learning travers, the horse must be competent and comfortable with shoulder-in and shoulder-out, and reliably obedient to leg aids.

In travers proper, the important factors are that there should be a comfortably held inside flexion, and the horse should cross his outside hind leg over and in front of his inside one.

How do I ask for travers?

- To begin with, just walk down the outside track with your horse well in hand and comfortably flexed longitudinally at the poll.
- Ask for a lateral flexion at the poll with an open inside rein and support with the outside rein on the neck.
- Put your inside seat bone and shoulder a little forward, and your outside leg back slightly, asking him to move his hind feet in just a little bit off the track, along which you look.
- Say 'good boy', and after a stride or two to give him the feel of it, release the aids and let the horse straighten his hindquarters again.
- On the left rein, walk a 10m circle in a corner of the school, using position left, and as the forefeet come on to the track, slightly exaggerate your position left and weight your left seat bone.
- Look along the track and nudge the horse up the track with your outside leg (just behind the girth) and rein.
- The inside rein is open and inviting whilst maintaining the flexion, and the inside leg also asks for bend and movement.

Ask for only a gentle angle and be delighted with even one step. Praise the horse instantly and profusely for success. To come out of travers, straighten your aids and the horse will naturally straighten on to the track.

69 About renvers

Like travers, renvers accustoms the horse to travelling flexed and looking where he is going; it is therefore an excellent introduction to half-pass. It also supples and strengthens the horse, and makes him responsive to precise positioning by the rider, which makes him think about the aids. Many believe that renvers is more difficult than travers, and should be taught after it.

About renvers

Renvers (pronounced *ron-vair*) is performed with the tail to the wall, the horse flexed in the direction of movement, looking where he is going, because it is not one of the SO.SI. LY movements. You can remember it by thinking R for renvers, R for rump – rump to the wall = renvers.

Again, renvers is an excellent strengthening and suppling exercise, and a good lead-in to half-pass. Horses need to be obedient and supple for renvers, and should be accomplished at their earlier work. I believe that they do find renvers a little more difficult than travers, although it is just travers the other way round. This may be because horses naturally seem to want to go with their shoulders near the fence.

(This can be seen in horses on the straight: their shoulders are slightly narrower than their hips and this often means that they line up their outsides with the fence but their insides are necessarily slanted inwards and their inside fore hoof lands fractionally in from the inside hind.)

How do I ask for renvers?

- Firstly, ride your horse well in hand and softly flexed longitudinally at the poll, straight along the track.
- Carry both hands slightly to the inside to move the forehand a touch in, supported with your outside leg tapping at the girth. Your outside rein will press sideways against the neck, and the inside one will open in invitation.
- Keep looking down the track, and open the fingers of the hand away from the fence, then ask for a slight flexion towards the fence with the hand nearest it. Immediately say 'good boy', release the aids, and allow the horse to straighten his forehand.
- One simple way to go into renvers is to ride straight down the track, say, on the right rein, in a well-in-hand, ordinary walk, with the horse stepping well forward behind.
- Turn his forehand off the track just as above, but ask for a little more angle.
- Put your left seat bone forward and

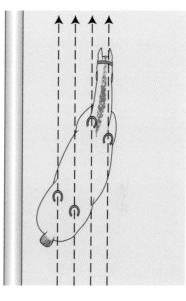

weight it a little, and have your right leg just behind the girth.
- Then ask for your gentle left flexion with an open left rein, pulse the right rein against the neck just in front of the withers, and tap the right leg against the horse.
- Look up the track and sit tall and soft – and you'll get left renvers. Say 'good boy' the instant you do.

70 Aim for half-pass

For these next two topics, even though this book is about basic schooling, I thought it would be exciting to think about some more advanced work. I've chosen half-pass because it is quite attainable with application, and canter pirouette because it is so often done poorly, even at high levels of competition.

About half-pass

As you will have gathered from travers and renvers, these two movements prepare horse and rider for half-pass, which could be described as a more demanding version of them. In all of them, the horse is flexed in the direction of movement and looks the way he is going.

However, half-pass demands greater collection from the horse (and so strength and balance) and the outside legs must cross definitely in front of and past the inside ones, which they cannot do without true engagement behind and lift in front. Because the horse is bent and looking in the direction of movement, the outside of his body will be subject to stretching forces which are exacerbated as the outside legs cross over, particularly the outside hind which is the main propulsive force. The neck has to be carried (correctly) higher and more arched, and the horse needs to be truly *and comfortably* collected and accepting the bit/s.

A forced and pulled-back head carriage, as so often seen, results in distress and maybe even pain, stiffness, no vertebral bow to speak of as the back will unavoidably sink, therefore no spring and flow. If the horse is at all on the forehand or unable to lift and arch himself up and back, he will be unable to perform half-pass, and forcing him to do so, or indeed any movement for which he is not ready, is abusing him.

How do you start half-pass?

If the horse has the pre-requisites in place, and can perform travers and renvers competently and fluently, start on the centre line and half-pass towards the fence, which the horse will find easier.

- Come down one long side on, say, the left rein, and walk a half 10m circle at the end to bring you on the centre line. Sit tall and soft, emphasize your position left, and ask the horse for a left flexion and bend, also making sure he is responding to your requests with your inside leg for ample impulsion.
- Look towards the quarter marker and, with your left seat bone and shoulder forwards, nudge the horse over towards it with your outside rein and leg. Allow the shoulders to lead, but do *not* let the inside shoulder fall off so that all you are doing is walking in a straight diagonal line.
- Don't expect too many steps, and praise the horse instantly for success; repeat on the other rein.

71 Think seriously about canter pirouette

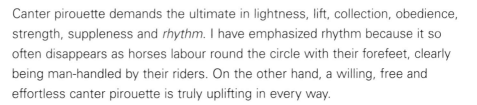

Canter pirouette demands the ultimate in lightness, lift, collection, obedience, strength, suppleness and *rhythm*. I have emphasized rhythm because it so often disappears as horses labour round the circle with their forefeet, clearly being man-handled by their riders. On the other hand, a willing, free and effortless canter pirouette is truly uplifting in every way.

About canter pirouette

First, refresh your memory about pirouette in general by re-reading topic 64 (see p. 99). The canter pirouette is done according to the same principles, but in canter – which, of course, makes it so much more difficult.

Before you think of attempting canter pirouette, the horse must be:

- completely able to collect fully in canter;
- be totally light to the rider's leg, rein and body aids;
- tuned in to her mind and vision aids – unless you want a purely mechanistic movement without soul; and…
- …strengthened and suppled by correct gymnastic work.
- He needs to have gone through all his previous work very well indeed, be able to canter a 10m circle in excellent collection, have rearward balance (forehand lift) and freedom with hind-leg activity, and be willing to be placed, step by step, by his rider.

Where placing each step is concerned, there is a fine line between placing each step and, on either side of that line, allowing it all to drop earthwards or, conversely, having the forehand spin around, which is easier than precisely stepping round in correct posture for the movement.

How do you start canter pirouette?

One good way is as follows (see right):

- Take, say, the left rein, and canter in excellent collection and with a slight inside flexion down a long side.
- Sit tall with your upper body and allow your seat and legs to drop lightly around your horse. With your inside leg, aim for that power-boat feeling with everything coming up and forward under your seat in front of you.
- At the end of the long side, softly exaggerate your upright posture and position left, weighting your left seat bone. Look back towards the quarter marker you have just passed and imagine the pair of you cantering back towards it as you push your horse gently but clearly round with your outside aids, and invite him round with your open inside rein.

- On the turn, a correctly prepared horse will almost certainly give two or three sideways steps with his forelegs – but don't force it.
- Say 'good boy', then allow him to straighten up as he reaches the track, return to trot, and make a fuss of him.

This movement can be practised carefully, with the rider maintaining the activity of the hind legs, particularly the inside hind, with her inside leg, so that the whole thing doesn't completely lose impulsion and grind to a halt! Take your time and, of course, seek the help of a competent, empathetic teacher.

Working with poles

Make the most of poles

Some people successfully school their horses without ever using poles, claiming that they have an inbuilt aversion to 'leaving the ground', even over a pole; but others use them all the time.

There is no doubt that poles, either flat on the ground or slightly raised at one or both ends, can be a big help in schooling, both in flatwork and as a preparation for jumping. They can help tremendously in making a horse's gaits and individual strides more regular, in developing his mental and physical agility, in the shortening and lengthening of his stride from collection to extension, and even in lateral work.

As an introduction to, and preparation for jumping, they are indispensable. From a single pole to complete courses of poles simulating various jumps, they are wonderful for novice horses and riders, and also for those who have lost their nerve or have never developed a correct way of going.

The best poles to use, normally, are rounded, heavy poles about 12ft (3.6m) long. No one has yet, to my knowledge, come up with a better material to fulfil all these requirements than wood. Although heavy poles are much more effort to drag and lift around, they are safe to use. Lightweight poles can be dangerous because they are so easily knocked out of place when horses hit them, can hurt them, trip them up if they do move or roll, and could even bring them down, any of which could seriously damage their confidence.

A safety note of a different kind: make very sure that your poles are of solid, sound wood, and are not soft or rotten, because these can collapse if trodden on, and splinter and cause injuries. Also see that there are no nails, screws or bolts which could injure your horse or, if using logs, no sawn-off ends of branches or other sharp pieces protruding.

A selection of differently marked poles is very useful. Suitable tree branches can be used as long as they are made safe. Plain rustic poles and plain white ones are basic equipment, but poles painted in segments of several different colours, not only white and one other colour, and poles with a variety of patterns, should all be used to get horses used to different colours and markings.

Although it is now generally agreed that horses are not colour blind, even scientists still do not fully agree on what colours they can see, or whether they see colour as we do at all. Some horses are reported to be frightened of yellow, and others of black. When poles are laid out on the ground, some horses negotiate a line of same-coloured poles with no hassle, but baulk at different coloured poles laid one after the other.

If working with poles is new to you, it's a good plan to scatter half a dozen or so on the ground in your proposed schooling area, and see how your horse reacts to different colours, and even to poles laid out in different patterns. If he spooks, you might find it helpful to read topic 94 (*see* p. 140) before you start working with them. No horse will learn anything if he is not calm, and you do need a calm introduction, especially to new work, if the horse is to make a good start.

72 Things to try with a single pole

How many poles do you need? As many as you can get hold of, is a good answer, but six is a minimum number for convenience and effect. However, what if you have only one? Is there anything at all useful you can do with a single pole? There are several things actually, and you're sure to think of other uses for one pole in addition to those described here.

Lungeing and long-reining Although young horses should be used to seeing poles about the place on an everyday basis, they may take a different view of them when they come into their working regime. Start by placing your pole on the ground somewhere in the middle of the school. Have your coiled rein/s in your hand and walk calmly and confidently into the school, all the time watching your horse's reaction. Walking between him and the pole so that if he does shy away he won't flatten you, gradually get him closer to the pole, walk over it yourself, lead him over it and finally lunge and/or long-rein him over it till he is calm. Move it to different positions.

Standing for mounting Many horses swing their quarters away when riders try to mount. Standing them against a fence can seem rather threatening to some and may cause rearing and running back, but a single pole on the ground about 1.5m (5ft) away from the mounting block often steadies them and keeps them in place.

Circles One pole can help you to form accurate circles around it because you learn to gauge your distance from the ends and from the middle. It may sound more logical to use, say, a cone, but a pole makes you think harder!

A mini-jump Take your single pole and slightly raise one end of it, on either a plastic or wooden block, and lead or ride over the low end, gradually working up to the raised end. Then raise the other end and aim your horse at the centre, leading him over, if necessary – although most horses, having already negotiated one end, will go over willingly.

Turns on the forehand and haunches Turning around the end of a single pole helps you see how much drift, if any, your horse makes when doing these two basic lateral exercises. Start with his fore, or hind, hooves, as the case may be, absolutely level with the end of the pole, and perform the exercise. The exercises allow small circles, of course, but if your horse drifts significantly from the end of your pole, he needs further work.

Cones and a pole Placing one pole on the ground between two cones or upturned buckets makes a gentle introduction to the idea of jumping.

73 Make corridors to improve straightness

The classical trilogy 'calm, forward and straight' shows how important it is for a horse to be able to go straight before any further useful work can be done. No horse is naturally straight, they say, and, left to themselves, it is amazing how few will actually walk in a straight line, with or without a rider. What can be done about this?

Thinking about symmetry

Because no horse is a mirror image of himself from one side to the other, we should expect that uneven conformation or muscle development will make for wandering and wobbly lines in action. The rider can often correct this enough by sitting with her seat bones centrally placed (as if you are aiming between the horse's ears with them) and by riding within 'the corridor of the aids' made by reins and legs; but poles address the fault from a different angle, by getting the horse to think downwards to where he is putting his feet. Most horses do not want to tread on the poles.

What should I do?

This exercise works best if you lay out a corridor of poles away from the arena fence. If you only have two poles, for instance, it is tempting to lay them along the inside track, but most horses will follow the track anyway, so this doesn't work. Get as many poles as you can and create a corridor about 1.5m (5ft) wide – not at all challenging, but enough to guide him and make him think.

Walk your horse straight in at one end, guiding him with your seat bones, legs and reins. Look towards a landmark at the far end, and just ride normally. Gradually narrow the corridor (a friend on the ground is always useful for pole work) until it is only twice as wide as the width of your horse's stance. This will really make him pay attention and watch where he puts his feet.

You would not be able do this with a fenced corridor, of course, but ground poles are perfect for it. Walk and trot, and eventually canter your horse up and down your corridor in its decreasing widths, and you will be surprised at how much more careful your horse is in his ordinary work, having got the feel of 'enforced' straightness.

74 Space poles accurately for your horse

If there is one thing bound to knock your horse's confidence it is having to negotiate poles that don't fit reasonably with his stride. Although poles can be used to teach horse and rider more about the lengthening and shortening of stride, spacing them at significantly awkward distances, and then asking a horse to negotiate them at speed, even trot, can cause a lot of harm.

Finding out who your friends are!

This is another occasion when a friend on the ground is a great help. Heavy poles can be tiring to haul about, of course, and it is extremely inconvenient to have to keep getting off and back on to move a pole a very small distance, so a helper is invaluable. In fact her most important contribution will be to notice exactly where your horse's feet fall, and where, therefore, to place your poles. As we all know, horses, cobs and ponies come in all shapes, sizes, leg lengths and stride lengths, so a little observation and homework will be necessary to get accurate distances for your animal's walk, trot and canter. You could try and do this yourself by lungeing your horse in all three gaits, but inevitably you will find that trying to keep your eye on where his feet landed, and bring him down to halt at the same time, not to mention placing the poles, is all but impossible!

Call in your friend. Ride your horse in a straight line in all three gaits – ordinary walk and working trot and canter – on three different lines, and ask your friend to put poles at two consecutive points where, say, his right fore has landed. This will give you two poles representing one stride length, a stride comprising all four footfalls. This will do for canter, but for walk and trot you will then need to place poles mid-way between them to give you the half-stride distances.

When the poles are in place, you or your friend can either measure them with a tape and note the distances, or pace them out (which is more practical during work) and, again, note down the distances.

How many strides?

Taking an average ¾-Thoroughbred or Warmblood-type riding club horse of about 16hh, the following distances will be a fair guide:
- Walking poles are spaced at about 0.75m (2ft 6in) apart, which is one short human stride, or about three of your foot-lengths.

- Trotting poles are about 1.20m (4ft) apart, or one long human stride.
- Cantering poles are about 3.3m (11ft) apart, or three comfortable human strides.

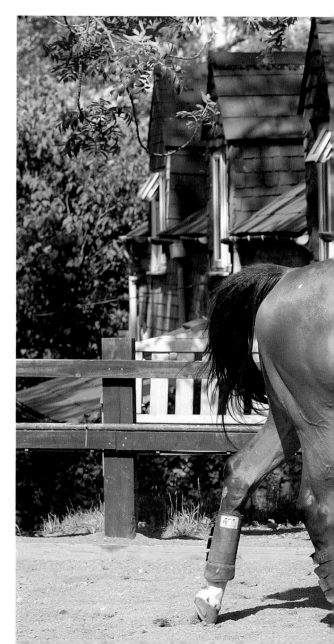

I stress that these are very approximate, and everything depends on your horse or pony's individual stride. These distances, though, will start you off reasonably well.

How to proceed

Take your horse over the poles, once they are set out, a few times to check that he is comfortable at the distances you have set. You can see the benefits of having lots of poles available, not to mention your friend, so that you do not have to keep getting on and off and re-arranging your poles for the different gaits, and the different qualities of each gait, such as shortened strides, lengthened strides, collected, medium, ordinary or extra-ordinary!

If your horse is new to working over poles, obviously just walk, trot and canter him over a single pole in different parts of the school first, after having led and maybe lunged or long-reined him over it. If he is on edge, a horse will not show his true stride, so when you come to use more than one pole (even only two) you may have to watch him keenly to space them accurately enough so as not to upset him further.

Be aware, too, that horses often try to jump lines of poles if they are not sure what to do. Slow, steady habituation is the answer, with a very gradual build-up in each gait. Just because a horse can trot poles with no problem, it doesn't mean he will walk or canter them just as well.

Most animals take to polework quite easily, however, provided they don't get any nasty surprises. Trick distances, such as were used some years ago (with jumps, as well) to 'make horses think', are not fair or good practice with young or inexperienced horses. Once your horse feels at home with poles set at his average stride length, you can adjust them to help him learn to lengthen and shorten his stride.

75 Use poles to improve all gaits

Many people use poles for trotting over, but are not always aware why. They may have an idea that the poles are making their horse think about where he is putting his feet, but the finer points of strength, lift, regularity of gait and stretching down the top line often escape them if no one has explained this. And trot is only one of the horse's gaits, anyway.

How can we improve a horse's natural gaits?

If you look back to topic 2 (*see* p. 12) on how a riding horse should go, you will recall that the horse has to work in a slightly exaggerated version of his natural posture in order to carry weight more comfortably and safely. He must learn to:

- raise his back;
- bring his hind legs more underneath him by flexing his lumbo-sacral joint;
- stretch his head and neck out and down in the early stages of his work, without going on his forehand; and later…
- …transfer weight more to his hindquarters, establishing a strong vertebral bow and stretching and arching his head and neck more up

and forwards with the front line of the face just in front of the vertical. Correctly carried out work with ground poles accomplishes all these things as well as improving

- thoughtfulness,
- agility,
- strength,
- forwardness, and
- lift.

How do I achieve all this?

By asking the horse to go properly in his approach to the poles and as he steps over them, whatever gait he is in (see photos below).

A give-away as to when a horse is over-faced by even a single pole is when he comes in hesitantly – he should look interested, calm and keen. Another give-away is when he cannot maintain his rhythm and impulsion over the number of poles you have set out (five to seven is a maximum) and you both lose everything towards the end of the line (see left).

However, much depends on your riding technique. Build up gradually both the number of poles and the gaits (starting in walk). Bring your horse in going well up to his bridle (accepting the bit confidently but lightly), with thrust from behind (generated by your legs at the girth), and control the speed in the approach with half halts.

As he strides out for the first pole, open your fingers to let him stretch forwards and down, and go with him with light control. You have to feel the fine line between keen, forward movement and contained impulsion and strength (both pictures, this page).

If he hesitates slightly, you have to give him confidence and encouragement. Use both your legs at the girth to encourage him forwards, and give a vocal command for the gait he is in – 'walk on', 'terr-ot' or 'trot on' or 'can-ter'.

Shortening the stride

Once your horse is comfortable at his normal settings, teach shortening of stride, as he will be unlikely to have a balance problem with this. Lessen the width between the poles by *one pole-width only* and reduce the number to three, building up as usual. Half-halt on approach, sit tall, drop your legs and ask with legs then hands for your horse to come slightly more in hand, to warn him about shorter strides.

Lengthening the stride

When the horse can shorten, produce more lift, and also keep his posture, widen by one pole-width the distance between poles that are placed at 'normal' setting, and reduce the number to three, building up as usual. Half-halt on approach, apply both legs and contain the energy with your outside hand whilst allowing him to stretch a little more over the poles.

Praise the horse the instant he produces a good result. With poles, do not let it all go after the last pole: the point is to retain the effect without poles with your aids, otherwise you are not making the most of them.

76 Use TTEAM patterns, Zs and other shapes

As well as making corridors for straightness and working over the poles, you can make other shapes and patterns to get your horse thinking about his feet and his body. You can give your imagination free rein, provided you build up the difficulty gradually and use sensible distances and challenges. Some horses only need one bad experience to wipe out weeks of good work.

Pole patterns for control and agility

From a standard schooling viewpoint, using pole patterns to enhance your horse's mastery of figures and exercises is really useful. The horse has to control his movements, using the poles as both a guide and a challenge. You can use a line of poles to shoulder-in along, leg-yield across and teach travers and renvers, for instance.

If you make a shallow Z-shaped corridor out of six or seven poles, you can teach your horse to cross them at an angle and, going between them, to do part-turns on the haunches to change angle and direction, or to simply listen to your turning aids.

I am an enthusiastic supporter of standard police-horse training and TTEAM work, the latter standing for Tellington Touch Equine Awareness Method (*see* Useful Addresses on p. 150). There are other excellent systems (and some not so good ones), but there is not space here to mention them.

The well known TTEAM labyrinth or maze (see above) does several jobs. You can walk, trot and canter your horse across the poles depending on his natural stride length and flexibility, or go at an angle and across the corners. You can negotiate the corners using alternate steps of turns on the forehand and haunches. You can perfect transitions and obedience by walking the corners and trotting the straight parts. You can negotiate it on an advanced horse in collected trot, and on a really advanced horse using passage, collected canter and part-pirouettes. It really is a pattern for all levels.

Other TTEAM patterns are the star (poles radiating out from a central point) – see below – for schooling bend and lift, and the pick-up sticks (a jumble of poles 'dropped' on the ground) for teaching problem-solving, attention and agility.

If you have enough poles but no manège, you can lay one out in a suitable field, using poles with cones for the markers, and can tie poles on to fence rails in a manège to round off corners when loose schooling.

77 Create a course of poles to introduce jumping

Basic polework will teach control and lift to any horse, but by using poles between jump stands, you can build up actual courses of ground poles to simulate a course of jumps. These are especially useful for novice horses, ponies and riders, for those who have lost their nerve, or for horses needing rehabilitation after bad riding or treatment and who have developed problems.

Treat it like the real thing

An excellent way to introduce, or re-introduce, jumping is to use ground poles or tiny cross-poles and single raised poles in a simple course, via loose jumping and in hand or on the lunge. Even placing a pole on the ground between two jump stands says 'jump' to most horses and some may jump quite high over it! You need to introduce things gradually, as ever.

To create a simple course, you can work on a standard figure-of-eight pattern, maybe within another route simply going large around the arena. At first, don't even use jump stands, just lay out single, different-looking poles one at each end of the figure-of-eight and one on each side of each circle, giving you six 'jumps'.

Walk over these in a forward-going, controlled ordinary walk, then lengthen the stride over the course, build up to trot and finally canter. All this will help you both to see a stride, particularly in canter, at which point little cross-poles can be introduced. Keep it all calm, forward-going and fun, and concentrate on riding correctly, on rhythm and riding your track, not making a big thing of the 'jumps'.

Always approach each pole as if it were a jump, giving your horse a reminder with your legs to go forward on the approach, and praising him all around the course as he does well.

Introduce jump stands on one or two poles until all the poles are between stands. Also, create doubles and trebles of poles as the horse's confidence increases, and place two poles next to each other. You can create shallow ground 'spreads' by using safe matting or plastic sheeting held down front and back by poles when the horse is really confident over the rest of your course.

Try to lay out courses in other areas of your premises, such as different paddocks, arenas and so on, and visit friends' premises for the same purpose.

Basic jumping

Jump up to progress

Jumping is one of the more exciting things you can do with your horse. Some people love it and live for it; some do it because they have to for examinations; and others do it because they realize that it is a good gymnastic fun exercise for their horse, even if his main job does not involve jumping. There are also many people who would love to jump but daren't, and have found in the past that some instructors have pushed them too hard, too fast and too far, and they have lost their nerve – or perhaps they lost it anyway because of unreliable horses.

This book is for confident, good riders starting off on schooling horses, which is different from riding a reliable, schooled horse. If you don't particularly want to jump, I hope that this section on basic jumping schooling techniques will encourage you and convince you that, taken tiny step by tiny step and at the right pace, it is, like most things, quite a feasible proposition to become reasonably competent, able to start a horse along the road with a correct grounding, and even come to enjoy it. We're not talking big jumps here – about 60cm (2ft) – but it is better by far to be able to jump a wide variety of obstacles and in different situations at a moderate height than to jump higher and higher but only in an arena and in competition.

If you love jumping and are pretty fearless but haven't actually schooled for jumping, I hope, again, that this section will prove helpful and inspiring.

Jumping is good for nearly all horses: it adds both interest and gymnastic development to their routine, which can only be beneficial. However, there are a few who genuinely hate and fear it: in those cases it is humane not to ask the horse to jump. It must be horrific for a horse constantly to have to do any work that frightens him and which he hates. Find him another job, maybe with another owner, where he can stay on the ground.

As a trainer, how can you be sure that your horse is ready to start jumping training? As far as actually leaving the ground other than a hop and a skip are concerned, the horse needs to be reliably very obedient to all your aids, he needs to generally remain calm and to trust you, he needs to be going forward nicely up to his bridle and accepting the bit, flexing longitudinally and laterally at the poll and through his body, and also working long and low in horizontal balance with no problem (not on the forehand). A thorough grounding in polework should have prepared him for starting jumping proper.

As far as your own abilities are concerned, it would be a good idea to read about acquiring an independent, balanced jumping seat (see Further Reading p. 150). If you do not have such a seat you are certainly not ready to start teaching a horse how to jump, because jumping is all about technique plus confidence. Without the technique you probably won't have the confidence; and if you have the confidence but not the technique, you could well ruin a promising young horse, or set even further back a horse that needs rehabilitation jumping schooling – but as a good rider already I am sure you know that.

78 Understand ground lines and placing poles

Although taking any schooling procedure step by small step makes it easier for the horse to absorb, making his fences easy and inviting goes a long way in his learning process and his enjoyment. Using ground lines to guide your horse's stride length, and also making the distances between elements of obstacles comfortable for his stride, are two ways of helping.

Approach at a forward-going working trot, comfortably in hand and calm. The horse will trot over the placing pole, which will place him the ideal distance away to take off over this small fence, making what will be a larger-than-normal canter stride. Follow his movement by folding *down, not forward*, and pushing your hands in a diagonal line forward and down his shoulders to his mouth. Raising the hands up the crest of the neck, as is usually seen, has the effect of raising the horse's head precisely at the time when you want him to lower it and learn to bascule (round) over his fences.

Ground lines

There are two interpretations of the expression 'ground line'. Some regard it as a pole on the ground immediately under a rail or at the front of a fence (as part of it), to enable the horse to judge its height and depth more easily. Others consider it to be a 'placing pole' laid a certain distance before a fence, to control the horse's striding.

The most difficult and uninviting fence for a horse to jump is a single rail with no filler and no ground line. This looks flimsy, and its height is difficult for an inexperienced horse to judge. A ground line (a pole or plank) placed on the ground immediately below it gives it scale and substance, and it will be easier to jump.

Ground lines can also be brought out in front of the fence (about 30cm/1ft) (see right) or, preferably, another pole added at this distance so that you retain your original ground line. This makes your horse look at the fence, ideally lowering his head to do so, which you must permit, but whilst maintaining the tempo – in other words, do not let him speed up or slow down.

Placing poles

A placing pole is aimed at *placing* the horse at a comfortable distance for take-off, to teach and encourage him. For instance, with a fence of about 45cm (1ft 6in) high, place a pole about 2.75m (9ft) in front of its base, depending on your horse's normal stride.

79 Make and use simple grids

Grids or lines of carefully spaced jumps improve a horse's gymnastic ability and focus his attention, teaching him flow, rhythm and tempo. Gridwork should not be started till the horse has mastered pole grids and small single fences with no signs of hesitation. He needs to be physically fit and strong enough to cope with grids, so build up to them gradually and keep them low.

What kinds of fences and variations are best?

The basic 'learner' fence is the cross-pole (see these pages and next topic), but you can use other things. Old car tyres threaded on to a pole are inviting, single rails with ground rails (as used here), little brush fences, straw bales with a pole just over them (so the horse is discouraged from touching the bales), and so on.

Never use car tyres stacked on their sides for any kind of jumping situation, because like this they could risk injuring the horse: he could easily get a leg down the holes if, for example, he was trying to bank a fence, or half took off and changed his mind, or dropped a leg as he jumped.

How do I start making a grid?

Start with your normal grid of, say, six trotting poles, but make the last one a low cross-pole. Then remove one of the middle poles and replace it with another low cross-pole. This gets your horse used to trotting down the line and meeting different obstacles.

Now build up a proper grid, first using trot distances and later canter distances, also increasing the height – but take it slowly. Rushing a horse at this stage can cause long-lasting problems. A good multi-purpose grid could be gradually built up as follows: start with a pole on the ground, then a cross-pole (to teach him to pick up in front and be straight), then another pole, then a straight-rail fence with ground line (to teach him to listen to your placing aids), then another pole, followed by a little spread such as bales or tyres (placing a ground pole 30cm/1ft from its base), then put a final little cross-pole 3m/10ft away (which will create a bounce to finish).

Obviously, your horse will need to be familiar with jumping all these types of fence individually first. Gridwork is not the time or place to surprise a horse learning or re-learning his jumping.

Study the fences used in the short sequence on the right: all are inviting and useful.

80 Use cross-poles effectively

If there is one type of jump that always seems to do good and never harm (I know that's a sweeping statement) it is one constructed of crossed poles, or 'cross-poles' as they are mainly known now. Of course, it depends how the fence itself is placed, and its distance in relation to other fences, but this type of fence can do everything – it is genuinely a fence for all purposes.

Ways to use cross-poles

Cross-poles are normally introduced at the end of a grid of trotting poles, flat or raised. When the horse can negotiate six ground poles, gradually raise the poles one by one at alternate ends. This eventually forms a whole grid of crossed ground poles, which really gets the horse lowering his head to look, lifting his feet and, at the end, jumping straight over a little cross-pole jump – a shape with which he is now very familiar.

Build a low cross-pole fence as the first fence on a course to invite your horse in and start him off straight and neatly. A whole small course of cross-poles of different heights and spreads really helps straightness. Spreads should normally be the same as the height of the point at which the poles cross, for example 60cm (2ft) high and 60cm (2ft) wide.

Another very useful jump is three ascending cross-poles to teach a horse to reach up, fold his legs and stretch straight over a spread. This also forms a narrowing space, from front to back, through and over which the horse must jump. It need not be high, starting with 30cm (1ft) for the front cross, 45cm (1ft 6in) for the middle, and 60cm (2ft) for the back one, but is very effective. The photos show a cross-pole used to set up a horse and guide him straight to the next fence. This has side or approach poles, again to take the horse to the middle of his fence.

What are the advantages of cross-poles?

- They help to keep horses straight to the middle of their fences.
- They encourage the horse to lift and fold his forelegs because they are higher at the sides, and the horse will not want to bang his hooves or the fence.
- They are inviting because there is a low part the horse can aim at.
- They teach horses to be precise, because there is only one realistic spot for them to jump the fence.
- They neaten a horse's jumping style and teach him to fold his legs correctly.
- They can be made low or high, and can be a part of a double or a treble, and two can form a spread.
- A cross-pole can be combined with a straight back rail, so using all the advantages of cross-poles plus teaching the horse to bascule (form an arc over his fence).

No other type of fence does all these jobs.

81 Build your horse's accuracy and initiative

Riding an experienced horse who adjusts his own stride and jumping effort and who just has to be pointed at his fences to tackle each one correctly and accurately is a dream, particularly for riders who are not wholly confident when jumping. How do you school or re-school a horse to operate like this, though? Indeed, can it be taught? Or is it a natural gift?

Start right – if possible

It is certainly much easier to school a horse to do something in the first place than to re-school one who has developed problems – but accuracy and initiative can be developed. Apart from tackling the individual problems of horses who have 'gone wrong', the method is the same as for starting a horse off.

Many trainers, particularly professionals at the higher levels, believe that the rider should control every stride the horse takes and should decide his take-off point, number of strides between elements, and so on. At higher levels of show-jumping and eventing this is certainly a valid view, but when dealing with jumpers at lower levels – whether show-jumpers, cross-country horses, hunters or fun hacks with amateur riders – I believe that it is essential for safety's sake to have a horse who can judge his own fences, strides and take-off. If he can't, when you do eventually get into trouble and don't know what to do, you can have a serious accident. A 'thinking' horse, though, will be clever enough to get you both out of trouble provided you sit balanced and let him.

How to do it

The proven classical technique of working a horse within 'the corridor of the aids' formed by reins and legs, and adopted as a state of mind by the rider, is one of the very best methods of making horses accurate *provided that* they are responsive to the rider's aids. Looking where you are going is also invaluable. In training, approach poles on the ground, or poles resting on each side of the front pole directing the horse into the centre of the fence, are also helpful.

You can't beat riding over all sorts of small to moderate fences, hazards, little streams and so on to make your horse handy and clever. It's as true as ever that hunting or drag-hunting teaches a horse to use not only his legs and feet but also his mind.

In general, if you think in terms of *you* being in control of the speed and the direction (your route or track), and the *horse* mainly deciding on stride and take-off, you will gradually produce a thinking jumper.

123

82 Teach your horse about bounces

Bounces really strengthen your horse's muscles because they are hard work and demanding. As a means of developing jumping ability, therefore, because jumping requires power, they are invaluable. They also teach quick-thinking, nimble use of feet and legs, and focus the horse's mind on getting through his line of jumps. They teach the rider balance and concentration.

Introductory work

Build a single rail jump, with or without a ground line or take-off pole, about 30 to 45cm (1ft to 1ft 6in) high, and jump it two or three times on each rein, aiming, as always, at flow, calmness and impulsion, not too fast or slow.

Then build another about 3.25m (10ft 6in) away, depending on your horse's stride. If the horse has done the sequence detailed in topic 79 (*see* p. 121) or something similar, he should be quite able to cope with one such bounce. Make sure of it by progressing no further till he can do single bounces like this, maybe changing the look of the fences before adding further ones to the sequence. Be prepared to move one jump back or forwards till you achieve your horse's comfortable stride, to encourage him.

Next, add another fence, at the same height, and the same distance away so you have three fences with an initial jump, a bounce in the middle, and one to get out.

Bouncing on ...

Most horses quite like bounces, and from your viewpoint, you are not expected to ride without stirrups and reins and to remove your saddle as you go down the line, as they do in the services! All you have to do is control the speed, stay in balance, and let the horse rock beneath you.

When you and your horse are both negotiating this short line with aplomb, add a fourth jump, and maybe a fifth. The next step could be to take the fourth jump back to the third, to create one non-jumping canter stride between the third jump and the last, giving you a jump in – bounce – bounce – stride – jump out. Then you can raise the back pole of the final jump one or two holes, then maybe the front one as well, depending on how you progress.

The pictures on the right show a simple bounce line of easy cross-poles, encouraging for any horse and rider.

83 Teach your horse to jump on an angle

At a basic level, you should not need to jump your horse at an angle in competition, but this skill can be very useful indeed if you get into trouble, come at a jump too wide, perhaps, or, when you come to jumping off against the clock, if you need to work out a shorter route without having to push your horse too fast. This is where your flatwork, to improve agility and obedience, really pays off.

A word of warning

Even at higher levels, bear in mind that jumping any fence other than an upright at an angle is very risky. Yes, you do see top internationals do it, but it is not advised for anyone other than a highly professional horse and rider.

How do I start?

As with most things, by keeping it as simple and achievable as possible – in this case by simply walking, then trotting, then cantering at an angle over a pole on the ground. You can build up to a line of diagonally-set walk, trot and canter poles, then raise the poles very slightly at both ends and go diagonally down the line.

Start with an actual little fence as low as 30cm (1ft), and approach from trot at a very slight angle, making sure, by looking dead ahead, like Sam, at right, that you land on the same line as your approach. Jump this from both directions, then raise it a little until it is about 45 to 60cm (1ft 6in to 2ft). Make it inviting by providing a filler and a ground rail, and negotiate it gradually from trot and canter.

Eventually you can increase the angle of approach and landing to 45 degrees from both left and right in both trot and canter and from both sides of the jump. Alter the appearance of the jump and move it around your field or arena. Introduce more than one fence,

and practise landing on a particular leg by giving canter right or left aids *once you are in the air.*

You need to approach angles with a very positive intent, and *look* firmly along your line to where you want to go, as above.

When you are actually in the air, *then* you can look to left or right

if you want the horse to land on a leg different from take-off, and he will almost surely land on it and you can bend away on it to another fence. If you think about landing on a different leg *before* you take off, the horse will probably try to change before the fence, get into a real muddle, and you will set him back considerably.

125

84 Learn to jump simple courses accurately

Having a horse who jumps accurately as a matter of course is a terrific boon because you can concentrate on your balance, the speed and direction, and on making moderate changes to his way of going without having to fight to keep him on his track, as is so often seen. Jumping just one or two fences accurately is in a different league, though, from jumping a whole course.

Techniques to help guarantee success

- Do plenty of work over varied cross-poles, as these make horses accurate, careful and straight.
- Do your flatwork up to shoulder-in and shoulder-out level at least, and lengthening and shortening of stride – it is the basis of everything else you do with your horse, and essential for obedience and agility.
- Ensure that your horse is obedient to your speed-up, slow-down and directional aids.
- Ride within the 'corridor of the aids' made by your reins and legs.
- *Look over* your fence, and/or along your line to where you want to go. It's virtually infallible.
- Keep your horse calm and in a rhythm.

Setting up your course

Start whole courses at a lower height than your horse can jump individually: you are aiming for accuracy, not height, spread or angles.

The simplest, most basic course is a standard figure-of-eight with a possible outer course round the track of your arena (assuming a 20 x 40m manège). This offers you the facility of one jump on each short side, two or a double or treble down each long side, with an inner, figure-of-eight course. Make the figure-of-eight triangular in shape rather than circular, so that your horse can jump on straight lines. Bends can come a little later.

Vary your fences as regards type, colour, fillers, ground lines, cross-poles, rustic poles, brushes, tyres and any other safe materials you can find, so that your horse gets used to variety. Build up from something as simple as four fences set on the long lines of the figure-of-eight.

If you are working in a field and possibly with a view to cross-country as opposed to coloured show-jumping fences, use variations in the ground such as gentle dips and rises to develop balance and agility; however, do not site jumps here at first. If there are low hedges, or gaps filled in with removable rails, use these by all means, but check the ground on the approach and landing.

Start off with an inviting cross-pole or little brush fence, and finish with an easy, rewarding fence, too. Ride forwards with purpose, balance, and with enjoyment in your mind. Have your horse in hand, and utilize the 'corridor of the aids' concept and, most importantly, *look ahead along your chosen track to where you are going, not down at your fences*. This is at least half the trick of developing accuracy. The old concept of regarding the jumps as mere inconveniences on your track is excellent. Try to construct the fences so that you can jump them safely from both sides at this stage; this enables you to give your horse a lot of variety from a few fences, and from maybe limited materials.

Have in your mind a clear line for your course, and where bends are concerned, look well round them whilst riding the track. This will get the horse round, but if you find that he is cutting corners on to his inside shoulder and so adversely affecting his approach to the next fence, lengthen your outside leg to push weight down into your outside stirrup, support with your inside leg, and carry both hands slightly to the outside whilst maintaining an inside bend by feeling the inside rein. This should not happen, though, if you start really low and in trot.

The point is to start very simply, to keep the whole exercise calm and rhythmic, and to think and 'see' to your horse where you want to go; he will then be very unlikely to make a mistake.

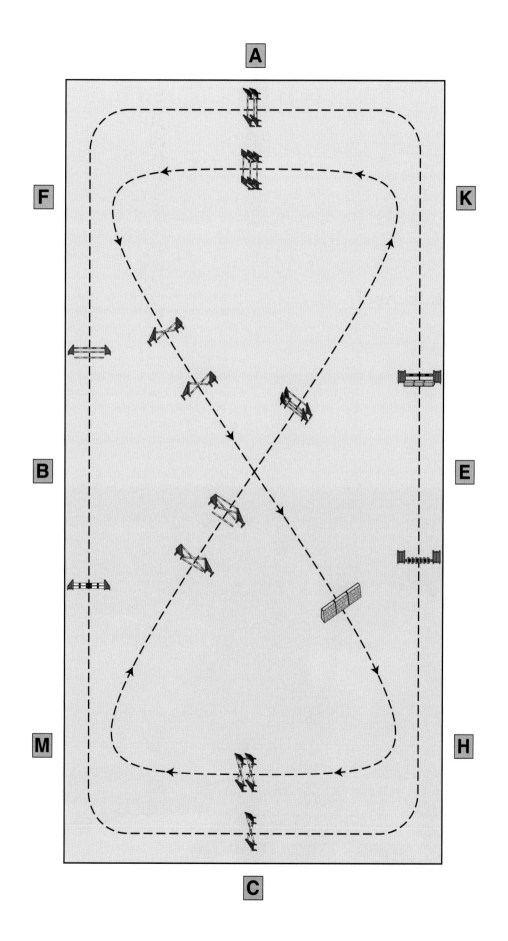

85 Deal with common jumping problems

Most jumping problems are caused by mental insecurity on the part of the horse. This can stem from lack of trust in the rider; bad riding causing confusion, poor balance, discomfort or pain; overfacing the horse; rushed schooling or incomplete schooling so that the horse is not established in his responses to the aids. In many instances, it is a case of going back to flatwork.

What should I do when I encounter problems?

When jumping problems arrive, then

- the rider's technique must be minutely examined, as many riders make their horse's job difficult (see p. 129);
- it must be positively ascertained that the horse is not experiencing discomfort or pain (see p. 18);
- it must be carefully considered whether or not the horse is being rushed in his schooling and/or over-faced by his obstacles;
- it must be considered also whether or not the horse is being jumped too much.

Using flatwork

The most important things about the effects of correct flatwork on jumping performance are that:

- it builds up the correct muscles, including muscles for jumping;
- it establishes reliable responses to the aids in the horse's mind;
- it establishes the correct way of going;
- it creates reliable self-balance in the horse at all levels. Self-balance is not an advanced quality, but is needed for good performance on the flat or over jumps.

Let's look now at basic remedies and progressive reschooling for some common jumping problems.

Repeated refusing

Any horse can have the occasional stop but when refusing becomes common all the causes mentioned on the left must be systematically gone through, maybe with expert help. Put it right and then, making sure the horse is comfortable, has a skilled rider (calm, firm and positive), and is presented with jumps well within his capability, try reschooling, going right back to pole work and tiny cross-poles.

There is a lot to be said for the old cure of a season's hunting or doing a different type of work. It is sometimes the case that a horse just will not work with a particular rider or that he has mentally 'burned out' as far as jumping is concerned. Some horses simply do not like jumping and if the latter two cases apply, there is no point in persevering.

Running out

Bad presentation at the jump is a very common cause of running out, as is overfacing and a rider who is over- or under-riding. Riders who themselves are unsure also cause running out (and refusing).

The first line of correction is to make sure that the

horse has a confident and skilled rider – neither rough nor insipid. This is often enough to change the horse's inclination to run out. When reschooling such horses, first try loose schooling both ways down a jumping lane, if possible. When the horse jumps well loose, try again with a well balanced rider in the saddle who will not interfere with him or hang on his mouth. Next, start with low, simple and inviting fences with side poles down to the ground to discourage running out. Initially present the horse slightly facing away from the side to which he usually runs out: if he runs out to the right, come in on a slightly diagonal line from right to left and look beyond the fence to your left.

Cross-poles are excellent for sending a horse straight to the middle of a fence as most will always choose to jump the lowest part.

Rushing fences

Horses who rush fences are worried about them, not keen to get at them. Again, all the causes given on the left must be considered. Rushing is not a trait to be proud of, nor does it necessarily show that the horse loves jumping.

Work out a programme of flatwork that will reliably establish the horse's responses to the aids. The problem usually lies in bad riding and/or poor, incomplete or rushed schooling so that the horse has never established the ethic of complying with the rider's aids. Once the horse speeds up and slows down easily and reliably, introduce ground poles and tiny fences, and maintain the horse's responses over them in all gaits, progressing from there.

86 Teach your horse about related distances

Although related distances may not come into basic jumping, it is as well to know something about this often problematic aspect of jumping, one that worries many people. Much depends on the horse's conformation, action, stride and speed, not to mention the state of the going, and the horse's ability to lengthen and shorten his stride promptly.

About related distances

A related distance is one occurring between two fences that are between three and five strides apart. More than five is not really regarded as a related distance. The implication is that although the next jump may not be part of a combination (a double or treble), it is close enough to be influenced by the horse's landing from the previous fence and the number of strides he can take between the two.

How can I build up to them?

First, you must make sure that your horse is reliably and promptly obedient to your leg and rein aids, and that he will (can) lengthen and shorten his stride easily and quickly. Cantering along a related distance to the next fence is not the time or place to have an argument with an unruly horse.

Having done your grid- and bounce-work, you and your horse will not be complete strangers to related distances. Get your horse used to jumping small doubles (two fences with one non-jumping stride between) and trebles (three fences with one non-jumping stride between the first two and two between the second and the third). Next, set up two jumps with three (see right), then four, then five of your horse's comfortable non-jumping strides between them. Pace these out to discover how many of your normal paces represent each related distance so that you can do this easily when walking courses.

The point is, of course, that when you jump in competition the fences will not be changed to suit your horse! This is where your stride adjustment technique comes in – flatwork again. Start by laying out at home, grids where the distance between fences is slightly shorter than usual, then slightly longer. Practise thoroughly over simple fences at related distances which are just a little tight and just a little long for your horse, and bring respectively your shortening and lengthening skills into play. You will need either to have your horse comfortably in hand, or to ride more strongly without, respectively, pulling him in from front to back or letting him flatten out of hand.

87 Teach your horse to jump narrow obstacles

When you get beyond basic levels of competition, either show jumping or cross-country, you will find that narrow obstacles appear in many courses. They are not always particularly inviting to horses, and they demand great accuracy and co-operation from them, plus direction from their riders. Gradually narrowing your horse's options is the key to success.

About narrow fences

One of the reasons that narrow fences are not inviting to horses is because they look higher than they are (a square always looks higher than a rectangle – it's an optical illusion), and it is easier for a horse to duck out to the side and avoid the issue – unless the fence is well supported by solid-looking wings or greenery to the sides. Then they often refuse.

Jumping such obstacles brings in, again, your accuracy skills (cross-poles help very much with this) and your horse's willingness to stay on line and go precisely where his rider sends him. This is, in fact, not a new skill, and it is fascinating to look at old photos of horses jumping happily over a single upright chair.

How do I go about it?

Even in recent magazines, there have been pictures of horses and riders with no saddles or bridles jumping over upturned buckets, a feat that shows a stunning degree of accomplishment. Needless to say, before you start your horse must have no tendency whatsoever to run out or veer left or right. He must, as ever, be obedient to your aids and easy to place.

Start by getting your horse to jump normal jumps, then try to find gradually shorter and shorter poles or planks, narrow gates, upright barrels and parts of fillers for wider jumps. Jumping a straw bale is a significant achievement, but don't stack them to make extra height as they can be dangerous if your horse catches them and sends them flying.

The top photo shows approach poles that have been gradually set narrower and narrower to help start the horse off. The bottom picture shows significant progress at home, as Sam and Murphy jump a narrow wall.

88 Teach your horse to jump corners

We are still on the 'straight and accurate' drill here. Corners always look awful to onlookers, but horses take to them much more easily than we might expect because they come well within the normal spread of which a horse is capable. They do, however, require careful training and a bit of imagination in their negotiation. They are specifically a cross-country obstacle.

What do you mean by 'imagination'?

An excellent piece of advice on jumping corners is to imagine a rail with one end slotted into the corner angle, and the other end attached to the middle of the opposite side, thereby dividing the corner into two; like this, you can pretend to jump the rail. Obviously it is essential to approach the corner at a right angle to your imaginary rail, and that you look ahead to a previously chosen landmark all the time during your approach and flight. Remember, where you look your horse will go, 999 times out of 1,000 – or thereabouts.

Corners need to be tackled like a mixture of a narrow fence, a spread and a cross-pole – in other words, dead straight, with attack (for reach), and with the horse lifting and folding his legs so that he doesn't hit the wider part at the other side from the angle, which could easily tip him over and on to his side.

How do I train for corners?

Start with poles set on three tubs or plastic jump-stand blocks, and initially make your corner sharper than 45 degrees, which is what you'll usually meet in competition. Start with a height of only 30cm (1ft), and ride it calmly, firmly and very positively. Widen the angle before increasing the height. Use rustic poles or safe logs,

and as things get a little higher, wider and more testing, put your flags in place to give the horse some guidance.

Don't jump too close to the apex because it's narrower, and unless your horse is extremely precise in responding to your placing aids, you risk a run-out. On the other hand, the

other end probably soon gets too wide to think of jumping it there. This is why treating corners like a narrow fence is best, and why your horse needs to be reliably obedient to your 'corridor of the aids' technique. Because of the spread effect, you need to ride accurately and very positively into corners, as below.

89 Teach your horse to jump ditches

Ditches are among the most unpopular and problematic fences there are, and it's really galling when you see small children and their diminutive ponies jumping them like Badminton winners! This, I think, tells us that any problems come from *our* minds, not from those of our horses. Children are notoriously fearless, and so, therefore, very often are their ponies. But where do *we* go from here?

You can't get away from it – or rather them

Ditches are everywhere – most hunting countries have plenty of them, hunter trials always have at least one, and there are great big yawning ones in British Eventing courses at all levels. Out hacking, many a horse and rider have been thwarted by a ditch, and have had to turn round and go all the way back again to get home.

Many fences incorporate a ditch in their construction: the dreaded coffin, trakehners, tiger traps, and simple ditches with a rail either behind or in front of it. Ditches can come with hedges in front of or behind them, they can have water (and croaking frogs) in them, or be dry; and, well, there are all sorts of ditches and combinations with fences.

How do I school my horse for ditches?

Ride him boldly, at any rate. This is most certainly an 'up-and-over' kind of obstacle, because if you look down into the ditch that is almost certainly where you'll end up. Your horse must be obedient and jumping other obstacles well before you start ditches, because you don't want a refusal. However, start on very small ditches as early as you can, so that your horse takes them as a normal part of his repertoire.

Whether or not you can construct plenty of different types of ditch at home, or have to go out and find them, jump them you must. Again, the hunting field, where you can get a lead from an experienced horse, will help if you're careful who you follow; or try to go on a park or farm ride, or a hack where you know there are little ditches, with such a companion.

'Little' is the operative word at first, as ever. Try to do a little jumping first, then tackle a small ditch and build on that. You need to ride really positively, keep your horse's head up, and *look up and ahead*. As ever, praise your horse verbally when he succeeds.

133

90 Teach your horse to jump up and down steps

Steps often look formidable, but, like other obstacles, they are quite achievable if the horse is well schooled and ridden properly. Gravity is against you both ways: it can pull you back when you're going up, and drag you down too fast going down, so a strong, obedient horse able to use his body well, and a self-disciplined, physically strong rider with a firm seat, are both essential.

How to start

Obviously, try to find just one step first. You should be able to make one at home, strong wooden railway sleepers being ideal. Make them at least two horses' lengths on the flat parts, and so that you can approach from both sides, too. Schooling steps of only 15cm (6in) are ideal, but try to make, or find, deeper ones. Start from walk going upwards, and, as always, take things gradually, all the time remaining positive, firm and strong. Progress from one step to two, which won't be a problem.

As you find more and bigger steps, your riding technique must be definite. Keep riding to instruct your horse. Approach in trot. Drop your weight well down into your heel so that you have some leverage and can push your body up and forward as the horse jumps up. Steady the horse well going down.

About steps

Horses find going up steps easier than coming down. I once became encircled by a rising tide on a beach on my four-year-old, and had to climb a long flight of steps to get into the grounds of a school, our only way out of a life-threatening situation. The horse never batted an eye, despite never having met steps before. Nevertheless I am sure he could not have gone *down* them so easily.

Steps are another obstacle that need bold and strong riding. It is absolutely vital to go *with* the horse up them, and not get even slightly left behind. Create lots of contained impulsion going up, and release it as the horse jumps up (see above). Going down, sit up with a strong, slightly forward lower leg position and control your horse's downward impetus, but without stopping him (see right).

In both situations, you should stay in contact without over-restricting your horse's balancing pole – his head and neck. You also must have a strong position in the saddle, with no flapping legs or flopping body.

91 Teach your horse to jump in and out of water

Water can be a real problem for many horses. Even a tiny ripple across a road can freak out some of them, and many go to extreme lengths to avoid walking through a puddle. We know what water is and, normally, how deep it is, but horses don't. The constantly moving, silver shine on the surface genuinely frightens them, and some simply don't like getting their feet wet.

him forwards till he goes. Really praise him when he puts a foot in or goes through. Repeat, repeat, repeat! The next step is trotting through and also cantering if the ground is suitable. Do the same with safe streams.

- If you can't create a pond at home, you will have to find courses or rides which offer that facility (see left). You can't become proficient at water if you never tackle it.
- Come in at a strong trot with lots of contained impulsion, sit up well and keep your legs rather forward (see below). Keep the horse's head up on landing and trotting through, then ride him strongly at the out fence or step. Do *not* get left behind going up!
- Always inspect the take-off and landings around water obstacles, and be prepared to wade in yourself to check the depth and the condition of the bottom.

Thoughts on water

Horses have evolved to depend on their feet for survival, and they generally do not like putting them where they are not sure of the footing or depth. Horses, of course, often paw things to learn about them, and water is unlike any other obstacle they are likely to meet. Horses whose 'play' fields contain safe ponds, or simply dips that fill up when it rains, may actually enjoy wading and even rolling in water.

How to build confidence

If the fields where you keep your horse have no access to water, you'll have to create a gradual introduction.

- Start by having a hosepipe running slowly across the yard, and let your horse follow an experienced one round it, getting closer and closer, and eventually going through it. Then ask him to do this on his own with his friend on the other side, gradually pushing him a little further out of his 'comfort area'.
- Ride through puddles, being aware that the horse will try to skip round or jump small ones. Hold him at it and push

Basic jumping

135

Hacking

Out and about

Hacking can be one of the most enjoyable equestrian activities you can take part in. Different countries and different regions of countries have different facilities for riding out or hacking. In some there is ample open country, over which the public has the right to ride (or walk). Some countries have rights of way – tracks on which they have a historical, legal right to ride – but in others, riding consists of hacking in prepared arenas or fields, or riding on 'metalled' roads that have to be shared with motorized vehicles. Some landowners may hire out their land either for one-time use, or charging so much a season or a year, so that people can ride in peace away from traffic, such as farm rides.

As a teacher of classical riding, it may surprise you to learn that I much prefer hacking to working in a manège! Although I love the intricacies of the techniques, riding, teaching people and horses, and get a lot of satisfaction out of it for its own sake, to me it is very much a means to an end – that being an enjoyable hack on a well schooled horse who is safe to take out in public precisely because of his education.

A lot of people nowadays, at least here in the UK, no longer hack, and some never have – and the reason is *always* that they say it is too dangerous. Sadly, this may well be the case if they have not taken the trouble to train their horses or ponies to accept the wide world without upset, or they don't know how to, or they cannot get any help from sensible friends, or they haven't bothered to arrange to ride out in the company of an already worldly-wise equine, to help reassure theirs and show them how to behave.

The fact that it is perfectly possible to 'bombproof' almost any equine is proved by the many working horses all over the world whose workplace is public space – roads, parks, busy town centres or quiet country lanes (see Further Reading p. 150). As always, it is all a case of doing things very gradually, in tiny increments.

I know you will be thinking: 'It's not me and my horse who are the problem, it's other road users. Drivers are crazy these days.' Point taken – but then think how much police horses and their trainers and riders achieve as regards becoming 'bombproof'. They work in horrendous conditions, but because of correct training they are as safe as possible. I once said to a Chief Inspector of mounted police that police officers must have an advantage because drivers wouldn't dare 'buzz' a police officer. But he said that, on the contrary, they 'skim' them regularly because they do not expect the horse to react. When training young police horses, he said, they took them out in 'civvies' because drivers were more considerate to them than to riders in uniform.

Depending on your surroundings, it obviously makes life safer if you wear high-visibility clothing, and use similar gear on your horse, at least leg strips.

Hacking is *not* merely a pursuit for those who daren't do anything else – much the reverse, in fact. To be competent at hacking you need to be sensible, road-wise, a good rider, and have your horse under control (well schooled) and accustomed not only to traffic, but to things such as trains, farm machinery, trail bikes, aircraft, dumped rubbish and so on. But the rewards to be had as a result of these qualities are tremendous.

Personally, if I had no other option but to ride in a manège for the rest of my life, I'd give up.

92 Spot opportunities for schooling

Many older riders can remember when the facility of a manège to ride in was a rarity, except for the wealthy or for larger equestrian establishments. In fact you can do a lot of good schooling work out hacking, both actual schooling exercises and figures, in addition to accustoming your horse to hazards, from traffic to loose dogs, not to mention riding properly – or certainly much of the time.

Flatwork

Of course, you don't want to go along with your horse going in hand and up to his bridle *all* the time; nevertheless, periods of this will not only do him good (see below), but may be required for control at times. Alternate between working or collected gaits and extended ones, or simply basic shortening and lengthening of stride. A hack is a brilliant opportunity to teach your horse to go along for significant distances in a long-striding, swinging walk that eats up the ground.

Use cross-roads and junctions to re-establish your horse's good manners by asking him to stand still whilst you are waiting for a gap in the traffic, not jigging and jumping about because he is impatient. Find out the local rights of way and permissive routes, and make full use of them. Use corners to perform turns on the haunches and forehand, use trees to bend around correctly, or practise your flying changes if you do them. Practise shoulder-in and -out down tracks, and use good canter stretches to lengthen and shorten the stride in canter and to practise transitions.

Jumping

Look particularly for hazards such as ditches and hedges to pop over, and banks and steps if you can find any. Fallen tree trunks with safe stretches (no broken off branches, for instance) are ideal, and woodland floors are excellent for teaching your horse to pick his way through going that is not straightforward, and negotiating gulleys that often appear in woods.

Use the terrain

Nothing muscles up a horse and gets him fit quite so well as hill work, both uphill and down. Going uphill in any gait is excellent for getting your horse to stretch down and forwards into your hand, for raising the back and getting push from the hindquarters. Going downhill brings the back end under and strengthens the shoulders.

Look for water to negotiate: provided you check that it is safe, it will bring on your horse's training in this important skill. Whether you live by, or box to, the sea, or rivers, streams and lakes, make the most of it both for fun and for his development.

93 Judge your horse's emotions

Misjudging a horse's emotions and behaviour is a common human error. I remember years ago watching film of a famous trainer teaching a competitor and her horse who was being very difficult. The trainer told the rider to hit the horse twice hard because he was being 'stubborn'. She did. It later transpired that the horse had had a back injury, for which he needed major surgery.

Responsibility

Out hacking there may be occasions when your horse indicates that he does not want to pass a certain place or go along a track because of some hazard. You must decide whether he is being awkward, suspicious, or is downright frightened. This is a big responsibility, because if you get it wrong and behave inappropriately you could destroy your horse's trust in you. Horses never forget, and trust is very fragile: once lost, it may never return.

How can I tell how my horse is feeling?

- If you can feel your horse trembling, you can be sure that he is frightened. Erratic behaviour with quick movements, head up, snorting and perhaps sweating, are all signs of fear (see top right). If his neck is hard and tense, he is probably frightened. Being rooted to the spot also indicates fear and confusion.
- Suspicion usually has the horse arching his neck, ears pricked towards the 'monster' as he investigates it with sight, smell and maybe forefeet. He will face it with his head, maybe snort, and swing his quarters around it (see centre left).
- Horses just being awkward or wanting an excuse to play up usually have some spring in their step, are quite relaxed, and they shy at familiar objects or situations. They seem to invent things to shy at, and give themselves away when they object to, say, passing a spot they are well used to *and which has not changed*. When familiar environments change, horses often register the change.
- Of course, too much energy in the diet, particularly from cereal-based feeds, and too little liberty and exercise, and poor vision, can adversely affect any horse's behaviour.
- The photo centre right shows a relaxed but watchful horse, and the bottom photo threat, anger and aggression with head down and ears flattened back. The horse's tail is also informative. A clamped tail means fear, a raised one means interest and excitement and a thrashing tail means anger or distress.

139

94 Learn to ride safely past spooky objects

It must have happened at some time to everyone who rides horses – and it could be anywhere. Your horse suddenly decides that something is waiting to pounce on him. He stops dead, swings his quarters around it, skitters about or, if there is space and you don't stop him, takes flight. There may not be a chance to get off and let him examine the 'monster'. What do you do?

The mechanics of a spook

If you are a reasonably experienced rider (and you need to be to hack out), you will have some warning that your horse has seen something ahead that has set the alarm bells jangling in his head.

His step may falter and shorten, and will become more springy. If the object is dead ahead he may stop and try to spin round and run back the way he came – or he may run backwards. If it is to his left he will prance to his right, and vice versa. He will want to keep his head to it (see right) so he can check exactly what it is and what it might do, but his hindquarters will keep moving, generally in a semi-circle round his head and the 'monster'. If he succeeds in turning a full 180 degrees around it, he may stop and want to investigate it, but he may then spin round on his hind legs and charge off. This is all assuming, of course, that you sit there and do nothing.

What should I do?

Act instantly to nip it in the bud! The moment your early warning system detects a change in his gait, and before the above repertoire swings into action, urge him forwards. *Sit up and stay that way.* Keep a decisive contact on the reins, and sit deep in the saddle with your legs dropped as far down and round him as you can. This all increases your security and your effectiveness to do what comes next.

The best way to get past the 'monster' is in a firm shoulder-in (topic 65, *see* p. 100) flexed *away* from it. If it is on his left, therefore, flex your horse firmly to the right so his head is looking away. Your inside rein strongly asks for right flexion, and your left one presses firmly against his neck just in front of the withers to get the head, neck and shoulders curved to the right. Your outside leg is behind the girth, and your inside one at the girth, both strongly telling him with rhythmic aids to *move*. Your weight is on your left seat bone, and you are looking up along your planned route, and not at the monster or at your horse.

Command your horse firmly to 'walk on', and keep doing so. *Only* when he does, say 'good boy'. *Do not* take your hand off the rein to lean forwards and stroke him.

Then what?

Keep up the shoulder-in till you are well past the 'monster'. As long as he is doing what you want, say 'good boy'. Once you are past the danger, you ideally want to go back and past it again several times to habituate your horse to it, and also let him have a good look at it; however, this may not be possible, for instance on a public road. If not, ride ahead straight, at a controlled working trot, if you can, and praise the horse.

Your taking charge actually helps and protects your horse and increases his trust in you, as well as your control and safety in future predicaments.

What not to do

What you should try *not* to do in these circumstances is:

- lean forwards (weakening your seat, destroying your security and lessening your control);
- raise your hands, flap your arms and loosen the reins so that there is no 'restriction' on the horse's mouth to prevent him going forward (in effect, giving him his head to do what instinct, not his rider, tells him – and without doubt he will);
- pat his neck to calm him, and tell him he's a good boy (praising him for dangerous behaviour, so he'll do it again at the next opportunity).

95 Avoid following a set pattern

Hacking

Horses, as we all know, are creatures of habit, and habits can be good or bad. You go out of the gate, turn right, walk for the first mile, turn up this track, have a trot, then a canter, walk just here, have a spin round that field, go down the hill, across this junction and home again.

But what if you want a change? 'Oh no, that's not what we do,' says your horse, and refuses to budge.

Variety is the spice of life

Apart from making your rides more interesting, taking different routes increases your horse's experience of the world and satisfies his migratory instincts. Feral horses have many square miles in which to roam, and although they have favoured areas, they change these according to the time of year and grass growth, or the need for shelter.

The trouble with only going one way all the time is that your horse may not be willing or confident to try something different. You need to get him used to doing different routes so that he takes it in his stride, and trusts you not to take him anywhere that will hurt him. If you don't, you may find that the horse starts creating no-go areas, and even decides whether or not he will go out at all. On a familiar route, he may take charge and go at his own speed, maybe even turning round and

going home if he feels like it. When you try to assert your authority, some horses can play up quite dangerously.

What can I do?

Work out as many routes as you can, and try not to do the same one twice running. Remember that even alternately going the opposite way round a route makes it seem different to your horse, so you probably have double the number you thought you had.

Select different routes for different purposes. You may only have time for a short half-hour hack, or you may be free for half a day. You may just want to do walking roadwork, or you may be trying to get your horse fit and need to find somewhere suitable for fast work.

If you can work out a combination of linked rides, you can vary your options greatly by linking up different sections, changing direction round them, calling on a friend or neighbour, and also not walking, trotting or cantering in exactly the same places each time.

Personally I love hacking alone – as does the rider on the left, or so it seems. However, you should always tell someone roughly where you are going, and carry identification, and your mobile phone.

96 Test your control

Related to the previous topic is this one of testing your control of your horse out hacking, particularly if you are doing something very familiar to him. You need to know that your horse, even though he may, we hope, be enjoying his hack, is ready and willing to go anywhere, at any time and at any gait, at your bidding; otherwise he is effectively taking charge of you.

Surely I'll know if I don't have control?

A horse who does not do what his rider asks is out of control, and a horse who is out of control can become very dangerous very quickly. It is surprising the number of people who do not see disobedience that way. Although carrying out a habit is not, in itself, disobedience or lack of co-operation – however you like to put it – when you ask the horse to change and he refuses to do so, unless he is genuinely frightened, that is disobedience.

Disobedience is, in some quarters of the horse world, a politically incorrect word. It smacks, some say, of dominance – our dominating the horse, that is, and instead we must aim for a 50/50 partnership. I believe that the most we can achieve, if we're interested in safety, is a 49/51 partnership in our favour, with *most* horses.

What can I do?

A fairly standard way of knowing whether or not your horse is acting out of habit or doing as you ask is simply to ask him to do something easy but different, such as trotting where you normally walk, jumping a ditch from the opposite side to usual, and walking straight past the gate into home and

continuing up the lane, rather than turning in (above). If he'll do all these things, you've no problem.

If any of these things produces an objection, just keep asking for and performing them, calmly, firmly and positively, until you can rely on your horse doing exactly what you ask, provided that what you ask is reasonable.

Competition

That winning feeling

Equestrian competition has never been more popular than it is now. To some people it is the only reason to have a horse, although the pendulum is beginning to swing back a little as more and more people want a horse simply because they want a horse and love riding for its own sake.

If competition is your interest, schooling will certainly be important to you. You can practise at home and out hacking until you are foot perfect, but if you want to compete and compare your skills with others, there comes a time when the only thing that will bring you both on is to get out there and compete.

It is excellent advice to have your horse working at a higher level at home than he will need to produce in competition. Only seasoned equine competitors are normally completely unphased by the excitement and buzz of a show or other event. There are the crowds, the music, maybe flags, the loudspeakers, the strange surroundings and, of course, scores or maybe hundreds of other horses and animals, all strangers, milling around the showground. All this pressure, plus a journey beforehand, is enough for most horses, without having to produce their best work. If you expect that, you will probably be disappointed.

Although if you are a serious competitor winning prizes will be important to you, it can benefit you and your horse to take a middle-of-the-road attitude. Even if you don't win a rosette or trophy, be over the moon if your horse performs well at first and, as he gets more experience, does his best for you, even if it is not enough to get in the ribbons. He can do no more.

Clearly, the only sensible course of action is to start small, perhaps by giving your horse outings that are not actually to competitions, but to friends' premises, to lessons or training days, so that your horse can get used to working in strange surroundings without the excitement and noise of a competition atmosphere.

When he is giving a good account of himself away from home like this, search out some small venues with suitable classes for him of a lower performance level than he is working at. And bear in mind that, even if you have paid your entries and are raring to go, if the weather conditions are really awful – scorching hot sun and flies, or maybe cold winds and relentless rain – then it's a good idea to give the day a miss. This may sound crazy, but a horse's first experience of competition needs to be good, or he will have a lasting memory of having had an awful time, and will associate it with other outings in future.

If you get to the venue and find out that there is something your horse will have to do which is just too difficult for his present level, small shows will often let you miss out a particular obstacle or movement and may also let you ride non-competitively (HC, or *hors concours*). It is bad horsemanship to push a young or green horse beyond his capabilities: he will do much better for you for much longer if you take it easy with him whilst he is learning.

97 Practise your test or show without boring your horse

They always say that you should not practise a dressage test or even an individual show for a showing class because the horse will learn it, anticipate the movements, and rush through it, not doing things properly and, of course, not acting in response to his rider. Of course, you do need to practise the individual movements, but not to the extent that your horse becomes bored, or anticipates what you are going to ask him.

Does it matter if a horse anticipates?

I always used to think that the advice to avoid practising a dressage test all the way through to prevent the horse learning it was rubbish, until I saw some circus liberty horses performing their act, to music, without any cues from their trainer. She claimed that the music acted as an association cue, and that they would perform acts from years ago if they heard the right music.

From a dressage or showing viewpoint, does this matter? Many think that anticipation is a sign of intelligence, others that it is simply a sign of a habit having been formed. It does matter, however, because when a horse does things of his own accord he does not normally do them as correctly as when given the aids by his rider.

What can I do?

If you are worried by this issue, the best thing is to simply practise individual movements, particularly your most difficult ones, and also sections of the test, but only run through the complete thing in correct order occasionally. This does also prevent a horse becoming bored or blasé. Nor is it a good idea to practise too often. So as long as you know your test and you work on your worst parts, you can easily put it all together on the day.

As an experiment, try learning a simple test you are not going to need, and practise it straight through several times, just to see if your horse has learnt it. My experience is that, without cues from music or his rider, he won't have done so, nor will he anticipate if you ride correctly.

98 Accustom your horse to a show atmosphere

There is nothing like taking a horse to his first show to make him behave like a larger-than-life version of his normal self. Many horses will be in a state of high excitement, staring around at everything, their feet on springs and their mind in orbit, when they first experience music, flags, loudspeakers, generators, trade stands and all the usual paraphernalia of even a moderate-sized showground.

Why do they get so upset by it all?

Simply because it is all something different, and to horses, 'different', whether at home or away, usually means 'suspicious' and probably 'dangerous', until they've been taken out and about a few times, and have gained a bit more experience – and sometimes even then they still find it all upsetting and confusing. This is how prey animals think. On a showground, where they may never have been before, *everything* is new and different, and it all seems to be coming at them at once. No wonder they sometimes get thoroughly upset and anxious about it all.

What can I do?

A good plan is to organize a 'mock' show, either at home or at a friend's place. Get a loud hailer and get a male friend (announcers are nearly always men) to make pretend commentaries. Rig up a CD player for music. Try to get some bunting or coloured material fixed on clothes lines hanging about, balloons tied around, a course of jumps set up and 'rings' taped off in a field. And you could invite other horses and riders to attend, too.

Wear your showing clothes and numbers, plait up your horse and use his showing tack. Get friends to act as mock judges and stewards, and in general, make things as lifelike as you can. In fact, there's no reason why you cannot actually have a real little show among friends. Keep praising your horse when he is good. Above all, award rosettes (your existing ones will do fine) to get horses used to fluttering ribbons hooked on to their bridles or poked into a plait.

Attend occasions such as riding club monthly meetings and shows; these are generally low-key affairs and ideal as a starting point. Then progress to other shows, maybe going along and doing no more than just riding your horse about at first to soak up the atmosphere.

It's always a good plan to go with an experienced, well behaved horse who will set yours an example, but if you cannot arrange this, careful preparation on the above lines will see you through.

99 Learn how to settle an excited horse

It's happened to all of us. Our normally well behaved and trustworthy horse becomes too big for his own skin at a show for no apparent reason. Normally he's good, but today – well, you wish you'd stayed in bed. Not only are his high jinks a nuisance, but they could also be dangerous – and they won't do anything for his performance in the ring or arena. What to do?

Why does it happen?

The previous topic has covered this in some detail. This sort of thing is more understandable when a horse becomes excited at every show, but it is very frustrating when it only happens occasionally.

With mares it can sometimes be put down to their being in season, but not always. With any horse, it may be that one particular venue has a bad effect on him or her, maybe due to a past upsetting experience there, perhaps with you, or when he was in someone else's ownership. Sometimes, though, there is no apparent reason for it, and you just have to put it down to temperament or mood.

What can I do?

There is something to be said for the fast-acting nutrient and herbal calmers marketed for this very purpose, although not all horses seem to respond to them as might be hoped. With some horses, their feeding regime is altered on a show day, and this can cause digestive discomfort and upset, which

in turn causes erratic behaviour. Something as basic as too-tight plaits can also certainly cause it, due to the discomfort or even pain.

If you arrive at your venue having done everything conceivable in advance to keep your horse calm but he is still on pins, try to take him a little away from other horses, ideally in the presence of a quiet friend, and graze him if his class is not for some time. Grazing gets the head down, distracts the horse with something he loves, and provides the soporific effect of grass itself.

When the time comes to tack up, try to keep your horse where he can see others but is not too close, and ride him around in a quiet, working rising trot on a gentle but definite contact. Slow his rhythm with your seat, try to keep your legs and seat very loose and your hands still but in touch. Talk quietly and soothingly, using words that the horse understands, though not all the time, as this can be very irritating.

If all this fails, console yourself with the fact that this can happen to anybody, and with some horses, once they are really tensed up, they remain so for the rest of the day.

100 Learn from the experience

We are constantly told that we should learn to be good losers! With horses, who are truly great levellers, we have to take the rough with the smooth with equanimity, and if we can't, we're in the wrong game. Every experience is a potential learning occasion, whether it was good or bad. Our horse learns what is expected of him (whether he does it or not) and we (should) learn self-control.

On a bad day

On the very worst of days when everything has gone wrong – you forgot your test, your horse left the arena and bucked you off, you had a massive score for your show jumping or you took the wrong course, the judge was your ex's sister who never liked you anyway and, to cap it all, it poured with rain all day – you can come home, put your horse away, have a bath and a stiff drink, and console yourself with the knowledge that nothing, but nothing, could be as bad as that ever again.

And what have you learned from the Day From Hell? Here are some suggestions:

- how to keep your temper;
- how to hold your tongue;
- not to take things out on your horse;
- not to kick the horsebox when it breaks down, because it hurts;
- that lots of other people disagree with judges' opinions, too, so you're not on your own;
- that your horse is still the best in the world and you love him to bits;
- that there'll always be another day – if you want there to be.

On a good day

On the very best of days when everything has gone right – your horse did the very best he could and never put a foot wrong, the judge wanted to take him home, you weren't sick with nerves, you had your first clear round, your extended trot would have put Anky van Grunsven to shame, and to cap it all, your horse won the Champion of Champions title – you can come home, put your horse away, have a bath and a stiff drink, and simply bask in the euphoria.

So what have you learned from your Day To Remember? Here are some suggestions: it has told you that:

- the gods do smile on you quite often;
- not all judges are incompetent or blind;
- you and your horse really are a pair;
- the smooth makes the rough all worthwhile;
- the hassle and the work have both miraculously and completely faded into the background.

Useful addresses and further reading

Useful addresses and further reading

UK

The Association of British Riding
Schools
Queen's Chambers
38–40 Queen Street
Penzance
Cornwall TR18 4BH
Tel: (01736) 369440

Association of Riding Establishments
of Northern Ireland
126 Monlough Road
Saintfield
Co Down BT24 7EU
Tel: 028 9751 0381

The British Horse Society
Stoneleigh Deer Park
Kenilworth
Warwickshire CV8 2XZ
Tel: (01926) 707700

The Classical Riding Club
Eden Hall
Kelso
Roxburghshire
Scotland TD5 7QD
Fax: (01890) 830667
www.classicalriding.co.uk

The Equine Behaviour Forum
Grove Cottage
Brinkley
Newmarket
Suffolk CB8 0SF
(Please enclose s.a.e.)
www.gla.ac.uk/External/EBF

Natural Horsemanship Magazine
Vowley Farm
Bincknoll Lane
Wootton Bassett
Wiltshire SN4 8QR
Tel: (01793) 852115

Horse-Centred Training
C/o The Barn
Mankinholes
Todmorden
Lancashire OL14 6HR
Tel: (01706) 839059

TTEAM – Tellington Touch Equine
Awareness Method
TTEAM Centre
Tilley Farm
Farmborough
Bath BA2 0AB
Tel: (01761) 471128
www.ttouchtteam.co.uk

Intelligent Horsemanship
Lethornes
Lambourn
Berkshire RG17 8QS
Tel: (01488) 71300
Fax: (01488) 73783
www.intelligenthorsemanship.co.uk

US

TTEAM US Office
PO Box 3793
Santa Fé
New Mexico 87501-3793

Equine Research Foundation
PO Box 1900
Aptos
California 95001
www.equineresearch.org

AUSTRALIA

Australian Equine Behaviour Centre
Clonbinane Road
Broadford
Victoria 3658
www.aebc.com.au

Further reading

Bartle, Christopher with Newsum,
Gillian, *Training the Sport Horse*
(J.A. Allen) 2004
Kiley-Worthington, Marthe, *Equine
Education* (Whittet Books) 2004
Lijsen and Stanier, *Classical Circus
Equitation* (J.A. Allen) 1993
Loch, Sylvia, *Dressage* (Sportsman's
Press) 1990
Loch, Sylvia, *Dressage in Lightness*
(J.A. Allen) 2000
Loch, Sylvia, *Invisible Riding* (Horse's
Mouth Publications, D.J. Murphy
(Publishers) Ltd.) 2003
McBane, Susan, *Bodywork For
Horses* (Sportsman's Press)
2005
McBane, Susan, *100 Ways to
Improve Your Horse's Behaviour*
(David & Charles) 2005
McBane, Susan, *100 Ways To
Improve Your Riding* (David &
Charles) 2004
McLean, Andrew, *The Truth About
Horses* (David & Charles) 2003
Moffett, Heather, *Enlightened
Equitation* (David & Charles) 1999
Paalman, Anthony, *Training
Showjumpers* (J.A. Allen) 1998
Pelicano, Sgt. Rick, *Bombproof Your
Horse* (J.A. Allen) 2004
Podhajsky, Alois, Complete Training
of Horse and Rider (Various
editions)
Stanier, Sylvia, *The Art of Long
Reining* (J.A. Allen) 1995
Stanier, Sylvia, *The Art of Lungeing*
(J.A. Allen) 1993
Stanier, Sylvia, *The Art of Schooling
for Dressage* (Sportsman's Press)
2005 (and any other books by
this author)
Wilson, Anne, *Top Horse Training
Methods Explored* (David &
Charles) 2004

150

Index

151

Acknowledgments

As ever, I wish to give a most sincere thank you to the team at David & Charles whose input on this book has been just as significant as my own. Their professionalism and humanity is always greatly appreciated.

Most of the photographs were staged by Abi and Sam at Barton End Stables, Nailsworth, Gloucestershire, whom I also want to thank for their terrific patience and for being willing to demonstrate both the bad and the good.

Finally, I acknowledge with humility all the horses and riders I have known as friends, colleagues, fellow students and sufferers, and clients, throughout my life. Even from

long ago, lessons learnt, formally and informally, come back down the years with amazing clarity and all contribute to the lifelong learning process. Many of those lessons have gone into this book and others.

All photos by HORSEPIX except the following:
David & Charles/Bob Atkins pp 43, 116, 118-119, 133, 144-145
David & Charles/Neil Hepworth pp 53, 66rt, 68
David & Charles/Kit Houghton p56
David & Charles/Matthew Roberts p82

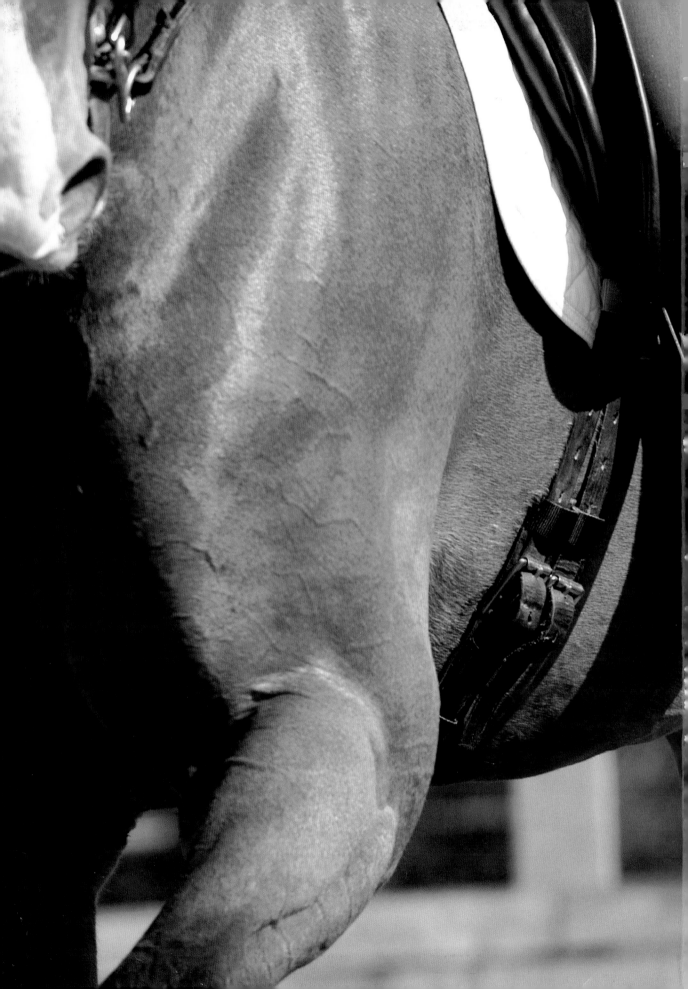